Lost Attractions

of

FLORIDA

Lost Attractions
of
FLORIDA

JAMES C. CLARK

THE
History
PRESS

Published by The History Press
Charleston, SC
www.historypress.com

All images are courtesy of the Florida State Archives.

First published 2023

Manufactured in the United States

ISBN 9781467145954

Library of Congress Control Number: 2022947981

Notice: The information in this book is true and complete to the best of our knowledge. It is offered without guarantee on the part of the author or The History Press. The author and The History Press disclaim all liability in connection with the use of this book.

To those to whom I owe thanks. Allison McGinley, Peter Larson, Paola Fernandez Rana, Darryl Owens, Joe Adams and Susan Patricia Scanlan.

CONTENTS

ACKNOWLEDGEMENTS

*T*his book would not have been possible without my editor, Joe Gartrell. He has now guided me for nearly a decade through five books. Adam Watson, Dixon Gutierrez and Katelyn Herring-Saltzberg of the Florida State Archives have once again come through with great photos. Laureen Crowley returned as the talented copy editor finding the things I missed, and Rick Delaney provided invaluable help. Wofford College professor Tracy Revels did groundbreaking work in Florida's tourist history and was a vital source. Rick Kilby's work on Florida's springs was important in preparing this book. I also am indebted to several internet sites, including Florida's Lost Tourist Attractions and Florida Backroads Travel.

1

THE FIRST TOURISTS

By the twenty-first century, Florida was one of the most prosperous states in the Union. It had the third-largest population in the United States and some of the most expensive real estate in the world.

It was quite a change.

When the Spanish first arrived, they were disappointed. There were no riches to plunder, and the Spanish were about to give up when they found two compelling reasons to stay. The first was the Gulf Stream, which ran along the East Coast, providing the Spanish ships a fast route back to Spain. Pirates waited for the ships and attacked. The Spanish needed an outpost along the Florida coast to protect their ships. They chose St. Augustine.

The second reason was pressure from the pope on Spain to establish missions to convert the Native Americans. Reluctantly, the Spanish settled in St. Augustine. They ruled Florida for nearly two hundred years without developing it. After the French and Indian War, the British took over for twenty years then returned it to the Spanish. By the time Spain retook control, the country was a third-rate power, unable to control the pirates and Indians. The United States acquired Florida in 1821, and the new territory began to attract tourists.

William Bartram came to Florida on the eve of the American Revolution. His book *Travels* gave people their first look at Florida.

Bartram painted Florida as an idealistic wonderland, and his writings inspired poets as far away as England. He described Salt Springs as the "blue ether of another world." Bartram helped create a mythical Florida. By the

Left: William Bartram was one of the first writers to come to Florida, writing about its beauty in the eighteenth century and inspiring dozens of other writers.

Right: James Audubon came to Florida to draw magnificent paintings of birds and helped promote early Florida tourism.

1830s, John James Audubon had come to Florida and criticized Bartram's portrait of the territory. "The representations given of it by Mr. Bartram and other poetical writers were soon found greatly to exceed the reality. For this reason, many of the individuals who flocked to it returned home or made their way towards other regions with a heavy heart." Audubon said Bartram was "causing a land boom in Florida."

Still, Bartram's portrait lasted, drawing thousands for the warm weather and the cures for every known disease, primarily consumption. This term was applied to various lung ailments, usually tuberculosis. Almost any condition lacking a cure was called consumption, which was indicated by a hacking cough—the graveyard cough. Doctors believed it was hereditary, and when bleeding and purging failed to work, they recommended warm weather.

In 1822, William Simmons wrote *Notice of East Florida*, which praised St. Augustine as a destination. The visitors came, and by 1835, St. Augustine had its first hotel. The town could accommodate about three hundred

JUAN PONCE DE LEON AT THE FOUNTAIN OF YOUTH.

The myth of Ponce de Leon and the Fountain of Youth dates from the 1850s and led to the creation of dozens of sites claiming to be the real Fountain of Youth.

visitors. William Cullen Bryant writing in the *New York Post* praised the town, although Audubon called it "the poorest hole in Creation." Whatever it was, it was difficult to reach, requiring every known form of transportation, from trains to the stagecoach.

Seeking the cure in Florida became known as "medical tourism" and was centered on the springs. There was not a disease the springs could not cure: rheumatism, indigestion, gastritis and syphilis. The myth that Ponce de Leon was seeking the Fountain of Youth led to the owners of every body of water in Florida to proclaim it as such.

There was a growing library proclaiming the advantages of the Florida climate, even though there was no evidence that the climate cured anything. Dr. Andrew Anderson brought his ill wife to St. Augustine and continued writing articles about the medicinal powers of Florida after she died.

In the 1850s, *Colton's Traveler and Tourist Guide-Book* recommended "San Augustine" for patients with pulmonic complaints, while admitting, "It is not only absurd but almost wicked, to send a sick man here for his health, when it is just as easy to send him to a better place."

The positive publicity continued with the publication of the diary of Major Henry Whiting, who called the St. Johns River "the American Nile." He wrote: "Invalids have long looked to

Poet Sidney Lanier was hired by the railroad to write about the wonders of Florida to lure visitors.

Florida as a refuge from the Northern winter, and during the disturbances of the last few years [the war with the Seminole Indians]. St. Augustine had necessarily been the only place of resort. When peace shall be established and the St. Johns reoccupied, that river will present many places of great attraction to the infirm and pulmonic."

Florida promoters bragged, "A Yankee tourist is worth a bale of cotton, and twice as easy to pick." Others used the phrase "Skinning the alligators," meaning fleecing tourists.

A *Harper's* magazine article painted a glowing picture and increased tourism. In 1873, a book, *Guide to Florida*, claimed that Florida could cure everything from asthma to Bright's disease to measles. The claims grew so outrageous that one book promised there were no insect or reptile problems in a state overrun with both. The Great Atlantic Coast Line Railroad paid poet Sidney Lanier to write about the wonders of Florida for $125 a month. He wrote *Florida: Its Scenery, Climate and History*. Ledyard Bill wrote the first real guidebook, *A Winter in Florida*.

2

THE SPRINGS

Residents of Jacksonville were surprised when the *George Washington* steamed into port in 1827, the first steamboat to visit Florida. In 1835, the army used steamboats to transport weapons and soldiers, connecting a string of forts along the St. Johns to the south of present-day Sanford.

The steamboat opened Florida to tourism, reaching the springs.

White Sulfur Springs on the Suwannee between Jacksonville and Tallahassee opened in 1843; soon, "sulfur" was dropped from the name. The sulfur often left an odor and was considered a negative in drawing tourists. In addition to hotels, the town had a bowling alley. The early visitors came from nearby Florida and Georgia, but soon the springs were advertised in the Tallahassee newspaper and appeared in national guidebooks. It remained open until 1950. Suwannee Springs opened in 1845 and soon became famous for its gopher gumbo. It lasted a century. Joe Hampton purchased a spring near Perry for ten dollars before the Civil War and renamed it Hampton Springs. He built the Hotel Hampton and promised that the water could cure skin diseases.

Clay Springs opened in 1800 in Central Florida and became Wekiwa Springs. (Confusion arises because of the difference in spelling and pronunciation: Wekiwa Springs and Wekiva River.) A hotel was built on the property but did not take off until John D. Steinmetz arrived from Pennsylvania in 1882. He took over the hotel and built Florida's first amusement park. It had a skating rink, toboggan slide, dance pavilion and bathhouse. In the 1920s, publicity for the springs claimed its waters cured diseases of the kidneys, liver and stomach. The land crash of the 1920s ended plans for further development. It became a state park in 1969.

Florida tourism declined dramatically during the Civil War because of local attitudes. The *St. Augustine Examiner* urged that anyone with Union sympathies be "hung high."

Feelings changed quickly when the war ended. In 1868, Florida established the Office of Commissioner of Immigration to lure the very people Floridians had fought just a few years earlier.

Green Cove Springs flourished after the Civil War, with ten hotels and the nickname "Saratoga of the St. Johns." When steamboat travel faded, the railroad spelled the end for Green Cove.

At the end of the Florida peninsula, Key West was booming, thanks to an economy based on salvaging sunken ships. Storms, pirates and enemies sent scores of ships to the bottom, many laden with gold and silver. It also attracted visitors, drawn by the warm weather and the excellent fishing.

Zane Grey, the famous writer of Western novels, came to the Florida Keys in the early 1900s and wrote a magazine article praising the fishing as some of the best he had ever seen. The article increased tourism so much that Grey found the area overrun and moved on.

The Timucuan Indians were the first to use the Silver River, making their camp at the headwaters and using it as a base to hunt. Silver Springs is at the headwaters of the Silver River and empties into the Ocklawaha River, which connects to the St. Johns.

The Timucuan Indians were displaced by European settlers, who came by paddleboats in the 1850s.

The steamboats were the commercial lifeline for the territory, bringing lumber and other supplies down the St. Johns, but the tourists wanted to see the natural beauty along the way and the clear springs. As one historian noted, Silver Springs was the Disney World of its day; by 1870, it was drawing fifty thousand visitors a year.

A major catalyst for increasing tourism in Florida after the Civil War was Harriet Beecher Stowe, the author of *Uncle Tom's Cabin*. In 1867, Stowe acquired a plantation on the St. Johns near Jacksonville, hoping to reform her son Frederick, who was a hopeless alcoholic. Despite failing to save Frederick, Stowe fell in love with Florida and began writing magazine pieces touting the state's wonders.

Famous Western author Zane Grey (*left*), with his brother, wrote about fishing in Florida, which drew thousands of fishermen and opened the Keys to tourism.

Her articles appeared in *Christian Union* and other publications, and she combined them into the bestselling book *Palmetto Leaves*. The result was a surge of visitors, known as Yankee Strangers. Hubbard Hart's steamship company paid her to appear when the steamboats came by, and a long dock was built so the ships could dock and passengers could get a closer look at the famous writer.

Above: Steamship companies advertised Florida cruises widely beginning in the mid-1800s.

Opposite: Harriet Beecher Stowe became famous for writing *Uncle Tom's Cabin*, moved to Florida after the Civil War and became an outspoken promoter of Florida tourism.

The city benefiting the most from the traffic was Palatka, on the St. Johns south of Jacksonville. After the Civil War, Palatka was "full of Northerners—invalids and tourists." Packed hotels led to a construction boom. While the sprawling Putnam House was the city's finest, wealthy northerners stayed at the St. Johns House, the Eggleston House and the Underwood House. When the hotels filled in the winter, residents opened their homes to guests.

After the Civil War, the ships began traveling down the Indian River, and hotels opened in Rockledge, Titusville and Eau Gallie.

Visitors jammed the decks of the steamboats. As they sailed along, the ships passed close enough to the shore that passengers could pick an

Former president Ulysses S. Grant took a steamboat from Jacksonville to Silver Springs. He is shown sitting on the deck.

orange from a nearby tree. One ship even had a bridal suite, and there was hunting from the decks as passengers shot alligators floating past or game on the shore. Stowe criticized the indiscriminate shooting. "The decks of boats are crowded with men whose only feeling seems to be a wild desire to shoot something." Still, it was national news when Annie Oakley was photographed on the boat deck shooting a gator. A first-class ticket cost six dollars and included meals.

In 1878, Hullam Jones invented the glass-bottom boat, allowing visitors to see the wonders below the water as they cruised Silver Springs. It featured water so clear that the fish appeared suspended in air. Guests could take the Jungle Cruise through the jungles around Silver River. As the springs' popularity grew, so did the attractions around it.

In 1925, W.C. Ray and W.M. Davidson purchased Silver Springs and began promoting the park and making improvements. They added gasoline power to the glass-bottom boats, increasing capacity. They added a young herpetologist, Ross Allen, who started the Ross Allen's Reptile Institute with alligators, crocodiles, snakes and turtles. In addition to the shows, Allen offered reptiles for sale. In 1939, you could purchase a rattlesnake for one dollar, a box of eight assorted snakes for ten dollars or a baby alligator for a quarter, creating the myth of alligators in the sewers of New York.

Between the 1920s and 1960s, Seminole Village, with Seminoles showing their way of life, was a major draw.

The Prince of Peace Memorial shared a parking lot with Silver Springs and told the story of the life of Jesus in dioramas.

Nearby was Paradise Island, "for colored people only," which drew about one hundred thousand visitors a year. It opened in 1949 in the Jim Crow state and lasted for twenty years. In 1953, *Ebony* magazine called it one of "the newest and largest recreational facilities in the South." One of the beaches at Silver Springs was reserved for African Americans. Admission was free, although swimming cost thirty-five cents, including towel rental and clothes storage. Silver Springs began admitting Blacks in 1967, although Paradise Island remained open on a limited schedule for two more years.

The first blow to the springs' attractions arrived with the railroad. Tourists were no longer limited by waterways, and the springs lost the steamboats, which had deposited visitors on their doorstep. As the number of visitors decreased, water slides and other novelties were added.

Critics began to complain that the area around the springs was becoming tacky. There was Deer Ranch, Santa's Land, Shrine of the Water Gods, petting zoos and amusement park rides. To make the Jungle Cruise more exciting, monkeys were imported from Asia. Chemicals and runoff seeped into the once-clear springs. Bruce Mozert, who promoted the springs with thousands of photos, said: "When I started working at Silver Springs…the

In Jim Crow Florida, Paradise Park was the version of Silver Springs for African Americans. It closed after the passage of the Civil Rights Act.

water was so clear you could see through the water from the swimming area across to the opposite shoreline which probably was over 250 feet deep. Today, there is a haze to it. The beach is gone."

Homosassa Springs was first settled by Indians some twelve thousand years ago. In the 1500s, Hernando de Soto explored the area. David Levy Yulee, the state's first senator, purchased the land in the 1840s. Yulee's plantation was burned by Union troops during the Civil War and sold to investors, who planned to appeal to northern visitors.

A railroad was built connecting the springs to Ocala and the north, which was the first blow to the steamboats. With the coming of the railroads, the springs began to draw famous people, including Grover Cleveland, John Jacob Astor and Henry Plant The trains made Homosassa Springs a destination—just a short walk from the railroad stop. It became famous for its warm waters attracting manatees.

Weeki Wachee got its name from the Seminole Indians, who called it "little spring." The spring is so deep that the bottom has never been reached. The Weeki Wachee River winds its way a dozen miles to the Gulf of Mexico.

In 1946, former U.S. Navy frogman Newton Perry came to Weeki Wachee and found it perfect for his idea of an underwater show. The spring was in poor shape, full of rusted refrigerators and abandoned cars. He cleared the

Weeki Wachee opened after World War II featuring mermaids utilizing a new system that allowed them to stay underwater for long periods of time.

junk and invented a way of breathing underwater from a free-flowing air hose supplying oxygen from an air compressor. People could stay underwater with a simple air hose instead of a tank on their backs.

Perry hired pretty girls and taught them to swim underwater with the air hose. He also taught them to eat, drink and perform ballets underwater.

In 1947, the first show opened and became one of Florida's most popular attractions. In 1959, the American Broadcasting Company purchased it and used its television network to promote it.

Hollywood discovered Florida's springs, which became the setting for more than two dozen movies. Silver Springs was the favorite, with six Tarzan movies, *Rebel Without a Cause*, the James Bond movie *Moonraker* and *Creature from the Black Lagoon* using the area in their shootings. At Weeki Wachee, *Neptune's Daughter* and *Mr. Peabody and the Mermaid* were filmed, while parts or all of *Airport '77*, *The Creature Walks Among Us* and two Tarzan movies were filmed at Wakulla Springs.

As with many attractions, the second blow was the arrival of Disney World. Attendance at Silver Springs and at the other springs began to decline. Despite ownership by Holiday Inn and S&H Stamps, Rainbow Springs closed as a tourist attraction in 1973 after corporate owners failed to turn a profit. The state purchased it in 1990. In 1986, Wakulla Springs was purchased for $7.15 million and became Ed Ball Wakulla Springs State Park. The county government acquired Homosassa Springs in 1984, and in 2008, Weeki Wachee and its mermaids were acquired by the state.

3

THE RAILROADS

*A*s the rest of the nation began to embrace railroads, Florida saw them as a threat. The state's transportation system depended on its extensive series of rivers, lakes and a thousand miles of coastline. Steamboats traveled the St. Johns and other rivers inland with regular schedules: from Charleston and Savannah to Jacksonville and other ports; from New Orleans to Florida's ports on the Gulf of Mexico; and from Tampa to Cuba.

State officials, heavily influenced by the steamship industry, resisted the railroad. When Georgia embarked on a railroad-building effort in the 1850s, Florida wanted no part of it. Florida could have railroads if they stayed within the state and did not connect with Georgia lines and the outside world.

The South learned the value of railroads during the Civil War. The North had twenty thousand miles of railroads, while the South had just nine thousand. The railroads in the South often had different gauges, making it difficult to move troops and supplies smoothly.

Florida was at a particular disadvantage. By 1855, it had a collection of short lines when work began on a railroad to link the East Coast to the Gulf of Mexico. The line from Fernandina to Cedar Key opened just as the Civil War began.

Although lightly populated Florida furnished few men for the Confederate army—less than 3 percent—it did play an important role in providing the army with beef. The lack of railroads made it difficult to get cows from Florida to the troops fighting as far north as Virginia. As the Confederacy ran out of money, it was easy for cattlemen to move their herds to southwest Florida and hide them from Confederate officials, who offered worthless money. The single cross-state line was heavily damaged during the war.

By the 1880s, there was still no link to Georgia and the North.

Henry Plant changed that, building a connection from Jacksonville to Georgia and the rest of the United States. He worked for the Hartford and New Haven Railroad until 1853, when he went south to establish the express business for southern railways. When the Civil War came, he saw his chance, creating the Southern Express Company, which became the primary carrier for goods shipped by the Confederate government. After the war, he began buying small, usually bankrupt railroads.

In 1881, he connected his Savannah, Florida and Western line to Jacksonville. For the first time, it was possible to travel from Florida to New York by train. He added the Jacksonville, Tampa and Key West Railroad, which took passengers to Tampa, then to Key West and Cuba via steamboat.

Plant began advertising aimed at tourists. One showed an alligator relaxing with a drink. As Plant headed toward the west coast of the state, Henry Flagler began his march down the east coast.

Henry Flagler became one of the nation's wealthiest men as a partner of John D. Rockefeller. He went to work at fourteen and, with Rockefeller, founded the Standard Oil Company. Flagler built a Fifth Avenue mansion in New York and was enjoying his fortune when his wife's health began to decline.

He believed that bringing her to Florida would help her recover. Flagler did not like Jacksonville, and the couple's stay was brief. Mary Flagler died in 1881, and two years later, Flagler married her nurse. The couple spent their honeymoon in St. Augustine. Getting to St. Augustine proved difficult, and the city was in a period of decline. But Flagler saw potential in the dirty fishing village.

A second trip in 1885 convinced him to build a fine hotel in the city and create the "Newport of the South." Along with building a hotel, he needed to develop an easy system for reaching St. Augustine.

For nearly a century and a half, there has been a debate over what led Flagler to develop St. Augustine. The best explanation may be that, although he and Rockefeller were partners, Flagler was largely forgotten. Building a grand hotel for his wealthy friends would be his legacy.

Flagler's grand Ponce de Leon Hotel opened in 1888 and was an immediate success. Tourists packed his hotel, leading him to build a second one across the street, then purchase a third hotel. Flagler created a model

Henry Plant created a steamship and railroad network that brought tourists to Florida's west coast.

Henry Flagler's magnificent Ponce de Leon Hotel in St. Augustine drew his wealthy friends to Florida.

for future attractions such as Disney World—creating multiple hotels with different price levels. The Ponce de Leon sprawled across five acres, with two miles of hallways.

Before the Civil War, there were a limited number of very wealthy people. The war created a large group of wealthy men who opened factories to make everything from cannons to boots for the Union army. Not only did these men have money to spend, but they were also anxious to flaunt their wealth.

Flagler purchased several north Florida railroads, including the Jacksonville, St. Augustine and Halifax River Railroad, and followed that with several more. He improved the tracks and created a direct line between Jacksonville and Daytona. Flagler and his wealthy friends could enter their private railcars in New York, step off in Jacksonville twenty-nine hours later and then change trains for a short trip to St. Augustine.

The guests at the Ponce de Leon wanted more than warm weather. There was baseball on the grounds of the Ponce de Leon, sailing and rowing races nearby, fancy dress balls—one held at the Castillo de San Marcos—and trips to the nearby beaches. On Thanksgiving Day, there was a football game between Jacksonville and St. Augustine. For the more adventurous, there were alligator shows on Anastasia Island. There were separate swimming pools for men and women, an archery range and tennis courts.

In 1893, George Reddington and Felix Fire assembled some alligators at Burning Spring and advertised the largest "gator farm in the world." They promoted the attraction extensively: "No visit to Florida is complete without a visit to this place."

Everett Whitney's family-owned Ponce de Leon Springs on the banks of the San Sebastian started in 1902 with one alligator—a longtime resident of the spring—then added a dozen more, along with bears and snakes. Whitney opened his attraction in November as Flagler's wealthy guests began arriving for the winter season. He promised to ride on the back of his favorite alligator then put it to sleep by rubbing its stomach. A large crowd gathered, and Whitney opened a second attraction on Anastasia Island in 1908. An electric trolley encouraged people to make the trip.

4

THE FIRST ATTRACTIONS

The opening of the Ostrich Farm in Jacksonville in 1898 and the Alligator Farm in St. Augustine brought a sea change in Florida tourism. The first tourists came for their health and the spring waters, and the second generation came to ride the steamboats, travel inland, see the alligators and the springs and enjoy the warm weather.

It wasn't enough to see an alligator; they wanted to see someone stick their head into the gator's mouth. As the need for entertainment escalated, so did the attractions. It would culminate with the opening of Disney World and Universal Studios.

While Flagler moved down the east coast, Henry Plant headed to Florida's west coast. Plant and Flagler were friendly competitors, and Flagler's hotel led Plant to build the magnificent Tampa Bay Hotel.

A pair of freezes in the 1890s showed Flagler that he needed to go farther south for warmer weather. He purchased the sprawling Ormond Beach Hotel and added a golf course, and visitors could watch automobiles racing on the beach.

From Ormond, his railroad pushed on to Palm Beach, Miami and finally to Key West. In Palm Beach, he built the Royal Poinciana, which offered tennis, bicycle riding, tours of Lake Worth for twenty-five cents and powerboats.

Flagler skipped Daytona, because city leaders were not interested in his plans.

5723-Acrobats far from their mountain home—grizzly bears in a street at Jacksonville, Florida.   Copyright 1905 by Underwood & Underwood.

Early attractions included trained bears in downtown Jacksonville.

In Palm Beach, he built the Royal Poinciana Hotel, with 1,100 rooms, and followed it with the Palm Beach Inn closer to the beach. Because it was near the ocean, it came to be called The Breakers.

As Flagler moved south, St. Augustine was left behind. The Alcazar and Cordova closed during the Great Depression, and an increasingly shabby Ponce de Leon Hotel closed in 1967. It became the centerpiece for Flagler College.

St. Augustine still had the massive Spanish fort to draw tourists, and it claimed to have the nation's oldest house, the oldest school, the oldest store and the Fountain of Youth, but Flagler and his friends had moved on.

Racing on the beach began in 1903 in Ormond Beach, and NASCAR was formed after World War II. Until 1959, the NASCAR races were held on the beach in Daytona.

Attractions followed the railroad. As early as 1895, Warren Frazee showed off his alligators in Palm Beach and Fort Lauderdale and finally opened an alligator farm in Miami.

Julia Tuttle and a few dozen others made up the entire population of Miami in the early 1890s. She had inherited land from her father and wanted to turn it into a resort. She appealed to Flagler to extend his railroad. There are many stories about why Flagler went to Miami. Many believe he always intended to go farther south; others claim it was the record-breaking winter of 1894–95 that destroyed orange groves in much of the state. Trees in the Miami area continued to produce fruit.

Flagler extended his railroad and built a magnificent hotel while reminding Tuttle that he envisioned that Miami would remain a fishing village. He continued with his dream of building a railroad to Key West, the Overseas Railroad. Now, tourists could stay in Flagler hotels from St. Augustine to Miami.

Jacksonville became the gateway to Florida. In 1900, there were 46 trains a day coming and going; a decade later, there were 152 daily trains during the winter season. By 1907, the city's population was close to sixty thousand. The crush became so great that in 1919 a large new train station was built.

Jacksonville's Dixieland Park claimed it was the Coney Island of the South and was the state's leading attraction for years.

Jacksonville became the center for Florida transportation. It was the starting point for railroads and steamships, and by 1886, the city had sixteen hotels, including the magnificent St. James Hotel, the first in Florida with electricity. The first souvenir shops opened in Jacksonville, selling ostrich plumes, statues made with coquina and alligator teeth turned into everything, primarily jewelry. There were casinos, saloons, brothels and opium dens for those seeking a different type of fun.

The city was also the entertainment capital of the state. At first, entertainers were working with dancing bears or wrestling alligators on the street. The Ostrich Farm opened with ostrich races—visitors could watch the races or ride the unpredictable creatures. A decade later, the park added a zoo and shows with dancing horses and high-wire acts.

Not far away was the Dixieland Amusement Park, which called itself the "Coney Island of the South." It opened with a long list of activities and shows. After a fire destroyed the park, it was replaced by the Southland Amusement Park. The Jacksonville Electric Company opened Lincoln Park, an amusement park for African Americans. Anything in the South with the name *Lincoln* was for African Americans.

World War I brought an influx of wealthy tourists who would have gone to Europe for their vacations. Two decades later, the situation was repeated with the rise of the Nazis in Germany and unrest in Europe.

5

THE HIGHWAYS

*J*ust as the railroads in Florida were years behind those of the rest of the nation, the state's roads were also lacking. It was not until 1911 that the first highway connecting Jacksonville and Miami opened. In 1915, the Florida legislature created the State Road Department, with limited powers. It simply advised counties and assembled maps of existing highways. In 1916, Congress passed the Bankhead-Shackleford Act, putting the federal government in the road business.

Roadbuilding was expensive, and the states needed to work together to create a network. The new law appropriated $75 million in fifty-fifty matching funds for states over five years.

Florida's first highway was the Old King's Road, built by the British from Colerain, Georgia, to New Smyrna. The road was built with crushed coquina shells following well-established Indian trails.

Carl Fisher, one of the most brilliant men of the twentieth century, was the catalyst for roadbuilding in Florida. He patented the automobile headlight, founded the Indianapolis Motor Speedway and opened the first automobile dealership. He was a champion of highway construction, conceiving the idea for the cross-country Lincoln Highway, then began the push for the Dixie Highway from Michigan to Miami.

Fisher sold his company and moved to Miami with his multimillion-dollar fortune. He found that John Collins had run out of money while trying to develop Miami Beach. Fisher provided cash in exchange for a portion of Miami Beach. He built a seven-story sales office and the Flamingo Hotel

The narrow Dixie Highway brought millions of tourists to Florida beginning around World War I.

Fruit stands could quickly turn into attractions with the addition of some alligators, birds or a garden.

and began selling land. Fisher's undoing came when he tried to develop a resort on Long Island in New York. He ended his life living in a small house on Miami Beach.

As the number of highways increased, the names became confusing, and in 1925, the government adopted a number system. Even-numbered highways went east and west, odd-numbered highways went north and south.

The eastern leg of the Dixie Highway became US 27, beginning in Miami and ending 1,865 miles later in Michigan. The Dixie Highway had two routes. One went through Indianapolis, Louisville, Nashville, Atlanta, Macon and Tallahassee. The second went through Detroit, Cincinnati, Lexington, Asheville, Savannah and Jacksonville. No matter where the driver started, the road ended in Miami. The Atlantic Coastal Highway became US 1 from Maine to Miami. US 41 ran from Cooper Harbor, Michigan, to Miami and included parts of the Dixie Highway's western route. US 90 stretched across north Florida from Jacksonville through Pensacola to Van Horn, Texas. US 27 first reached Florida in 1934 and finished in Miami in

1949. Beginning in the 1930s and well into the 1960s, it was the center of the Florida tourism industry.

At one time, there were dozens of attractions on US 27. They ranged from combining gas stations/restaurants/animal attractions to major tourist spots such as Bok Tower.

Tourism was on its way to becoming Florida's dominant industry, although the cattle and citrus interests still controlled the legislature. This meant that cows were creating an obstacle course for drivers. One publication warned drivers about the "roving razorbacks and range cattle" and pointed out that the state did not require a driver's license. It was not until 1949 that the state required fences to keep animals off the roads.

Thomas Edison and Henry Ford saw the sad state of Florida highways from their winter homes in Fort Myers and pushed for the construction of the Tamiami Trail linking Tampa and Miami.

In 1921, Kenneth Roberts, a writer for the *Saturday Evening Post*, was sent to Florida to write articles about what the state had to offer. He ended up writing three articles extolling the wonders of the state. The magazine was the country's biggest-selling publication, and its readers responded. Just as Stowe had done half a century earlier, Roberts touted buying land in Florida as a route to wealth and happiness.

The steamships had limited travelers to the waterways. The railroads had opened more of the state, and highways made it possible to go almost anywhere. Roberts told his readers that anything was possible in Florida with a car. You could come pale and poor and become tanned and rich, Roberts said.

6

THE AUTOMOBILE AGE

The invasion of the Model T Fords began.

The car could not only provide transportation but could also serve as a traveling hotel. A family could bring a tent, beds, canned goods and utensils. They became known as Tin Can Tourists. It is not clear where the name came from. Perhaps it derived from so many of them driving Tin Lizzies, or because they ate from tin cans, or for the tin cans of gasoline they carried. In 1919, a group of the Tin Can Tourists met in Tampa Bay's Desoto Park to form the Tin Can Tourists of the World. To show their membership, they soldered tin cans onto their radiator caps.

One observer watched the procession of cars and wrote

> *It squeaked and groaned, 'twas rusty worn*
> *Its fenders bent, its curtains torn,*
> *Its windshield cracked, its wheels not mates,*
> *Caked with mud of seven states,*
> *Headed South.*

Florida residents complained that the Tin Can Tourists were cheap. The locals said they came with one shirt and a twenty-dollar bill and didn't change either.

Given the conditions of the roads and the cars, driving two hundred miles was a good day. At first, the tourists had two choices: staying in hotels in cities or sleeping in their cars. The hotels were considered too

The coming of the Model T brought a new type of tourist: working-class men and women on a tight budget.

expensive; gradually, auto camps opened around the state. Sometimes, abandoned buildings were converted into cabins. They became more elaborate as tourism increased and eventually became motor courts and motels. In 1925, there were ninety-five auto camps in the state; a year later, the number had more than doubled.

The gas stations, auto camps and restaurants along the highway were mom-and-pop businesses, which gave them wide latitude in how they could draw tourists and market their services. Adding an alligator from a nearby swamp was surprisingly easy.

Finding gasoline was often a challenge. Livery stables and general stores began adding pumps. Gulf Oil was the first company to open stations in the South, and soon, its orange-and-blue signs became a familiar sight for motorists. Instead of gas being pumped into the car, it was usually sold in five-gallon cans.

By the 1921–22 winter season, Florida had nine hundred miles of highways on its way to three thousand miles within a few years. That winter, more than four thousand Tin Can Tourists packed Desoto Park.

Around the state, bungalows went up to house tourists. A fourteen-by-twenty-eight-foot bungalow cost sixty-five dollars a month.

Liberty Magazine featured a cover story on the Tin Can Tourists who came to Florida starting in the 1920s.

The automobile opened the state to millions who had not been able to afford a Florida vacation in the Flagler era.

The Great Depression started early in Florida. A pair of hurricanes in the 1920s caused widespread destruction in South Florida. The storms did not just destroy property, they also ruined confidence. Dreams of making a fortune in land vanished. Many had put down small deposits and could walk away from the land they had purchased, leaving tens of thousands of empty lots.

The collapse of the Florida land boom followed by the Great Depression devastated the state's economy. People without jobs did not take vacations or buy property in Florida. The state legislature, desperate for cash, legalized racetrack gambling in 1931, and months later the Hialeah track opened, drawing the wealthy. Two other tracks, Tropical Park and Gulfstream, followed. Dog racing and jai alai gambling were also legalized, and although they were not as popular as horse racing, every bit of cash helped.

The worst of the Great Depression was in Key West, where the city went bankrupt and was taken over by the state's Federal Emergency Relief Administration director, Julius F. Stone Jr. Critics, including the wife of poet Robert Frost, called Stone a dictator. But not only did he salvage the town, he also set it on a new course—as a tourism center.

In 1949, Florida opened the first welcome station—providing information and a cup of orange juice—where US 17 entered Florida north of Jacksonville.

In 1953, an effort to build a turnpike began. Florida's Turnpike opened in 1957, running from Miami Gardens to Fort Pierce . A second leg, from Fort Pierce to Wildwood, connected Interstate 75 with the east coast.

General Dwight Eisenhower saw the German autobahn during World War II and was impressed. He signed the Federal-Aid Highway Act of 1956 to build a national network of highways. The highways bypassed the small towns and put hundreds of roadside attractions out of business. Some attractions lured people off the interstate with billboards until 1965, when the Highway Beautification Act limited the number of billboards. It became even more difficult for the scores of mom-and-pop attractions to survive.

Interstate 95 stretched from Maine to Miami, and Interstate 4 connected Daytona to Tampa across the center of the state. I-75 followed the old midwestern route from Sault Ste. Marie to Miami, and Interstate 10 started in Jacksonville and stretched west to Pensacola, then to Santa Monica, California.

The interstate meant the days were numbered for the tourist courts and cabins along Florida's old highways. Holiday Inns went up at major interstate intersections, and other chains followed. Oil companies built gas stations at the interstate exchanges, and there was no room for alligators, birds or snakes.

7

THE TOURIST INVASION

*F*lorida went through stages of tourism. First came the sickly, looking for a medical miracle in the Florida sunshine. They gave way to hunters and visitors who came to see the springs. Then came Henry Flagler's friends, wealthy people who came to spend the winter season. They continue to come, dominating Palm Beach, as they abandoned St. Augustine and Ormond Beach. The automobile opened the state to everyone. Beginning in the late 1800s, the idea of vacations became widely accepted, and by the 1920s, millions of Americans looked forward to a week or two free from work.

For tourists looking for something new, a gas station with some captive alligators and free admission was perfect. Stopping for gas and a soda and spending time watching the alligators could create a memory to share with folks back home.

The alligators made the Seminole Indians stars. The Seminoles had a story to tell. They were the only tribe that never surrendered, hiding out in the Everglades until the U.S. Army went home after three wars.

Around 1900, promoters realized that the Seminoles could be a tourist draw. In 1894, Warren Frazee—appropriately nicknamed "Alligator Joe"—created an alligator farm in Palm Beach, and in 1910, he launched an alligator farm in Miami and began wrestling with the gators. It led the city—which wasn't founded until 1896—to launch a campaign to draw tourists.

In 1917, Coppinger's Tropical Gardens invited nearby Seminoles to establish a camp and show visitors how they lived. It was such a success that another Seminole, Chief Willie Willie, opened his attraction, Musa Isle Village and Trading Post. Both attractions featured alligator wrestling, which involved turning a gator onto its back and rubbing its stomach.

Edward Bok came to the United States as a poor immigrant and, through marriage, came to control the nation's largest magazine company, including *Ladies' Home Journal*. To repay his adoptive country, he built the beautiful Bok Tower at what passes for a mountain in Florida—324 feet above sea level. President Calvin Coolidge, a frequent visitor to Florida, came for the dedication. It is a US 27 survivor.

As historian Tracy Revels wrote, Bok Tower was "the first major attraction created to be a novelty, bearing no direct relationship to the climate, history, native people or natural wonders of Florida."

All along US 27, the attractions opened. Everglades Gatorland opened in 1959 by Mary Lou Bowen and her husband, drawing hundreds of paying visitors a day. Jim and Maudine Posey sold gator meat at Gatorama near Palmdale, west of Lake Okeechobee. The Cypress Knee Museum was a big draw, although it was just a hobby for Tom Gaskins. Pineapple Paradise in Lake Placid sold everything pineapple—pineapple toothpaste, pineapple wine and pineapple candy were the leading sellers.

A short distance away was The Great Masterpiece (Masterpiece Gardens), which featured a giant mosaic of da Vinci's *Last Supper*. Thirty

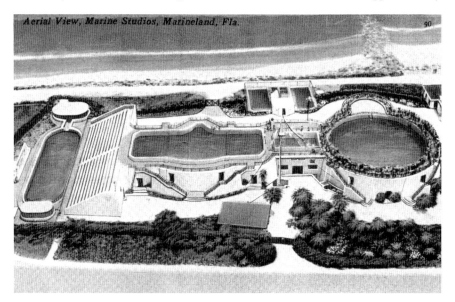

Marineland was originally designed to be a movie studio for filming underwater scenes.

miles north was the granddaddy of Florida attractions, Cypress Gardens. Circus World / Boardwalk and Baseball was a latecomer to the highway. Finally, the Citrus Tower in Clermont looked out over miles and miles of orange trees. Today, the groves are gone, replaced by thousands of homes, although the tower remains open to the public.

Even during the Great Depression, brave souls opened attractions. In 1936, Franz Scheer purchased a former nudist colony and turned it into Parrot Jungle. In 1938, Marine Studios opened south of St. Augustine with the backing of some wealthy men, including Cornelius Vanderbilt Whitney.

The original idea was to capture sea creatures and use them in movies—hence the word *Studios* in the name. Parts of *Creature from the Black Lagoon* and *Revenge of the Creature* were filmed there. In 1952, a porpoise stadium opened with "Flippy," who was billed as "The Educated Dolphin." The park's name was changed to Marineland in 1961, and at its peak in the 1970s, yearly attendance topped nine hundred thousand. A series of ownership changes, poor decisions and several hurricanes sent the attraction spiraling downward, ending in bankruptcy in 1998. In 2011, Marineland was sold to the Georgia Aquarium and then, in 2019, to a new company that changed the name to Marineland Dolphin Adventure.

Through the 1930s, the nation's economy slowly improved, and by 1941, it looked like Florida would have a record-breaking tourist season. The season was to begin on December 7, the day the Japanese attacked Pearl Harbor. At first, hotel owners worried that the war would destroy tourism, and gasoline rationing discouraged people from coming. Soon, Florida became one giant military base. From Pensacola to Key West, scores of military bases opened.

The Florida weather provided ideal conditions for training, whether for pilots, sailors or soldiers. They jammed the hotel rooms, including the Vinoy Park Hotel in St. Petersburg, The Breakers in Palm Beach, the Don CeSar in St. Petersburg Beach and thousands of hotel rooms in the Miami area. Smaller hotels and cabins were occupied by the families of those undergoing training at one of the 172 military installations in the state. As the fighting began, hotels—including The Breakers—were used as hospitals.

Two future presidents, John Kennedy and George H.W. Bush, trained in Florida.

Many Americans thought there was something wrong with taking a vacation in the middle of a war. Florida fought back with the slogan "Civilians need furloughs, too."

The end of the war in 1945 brought an unprecedented wave of tourists to Florida. Rationing and wage and price controls meant that most

Americans had been reluctant savers during the war. Now, they wanted to have fun and spend money.

Not only did visitors come; nearly a million new residents moved to the state between 1940 and 1950.

Florida now had three things to make its future secure. First, the window air conditioner meant that people no longer had to suffer through miserable summers. More than that, it meant that hundreds of thousands of cheap, cinderblock homes could be built with an air conditioner inserted into a hole in the wall. No longer did home builders have to erect residences designed to allow breezes to cool the home.

The second factor was Social Security. It allowed people to retire to Florida with a guaranteed source of income. Retirees could sell their homes in the North, buy a cheaper home in Florida and live comfortably.

Finally, bringing the mosquitoes under control eliminated one of the most unpleasant parts of living in Florida. A spray using DDT was developed in Florida during the war, and trucks spraying what would later turn out to be a dangerous substance were everywhere.

After the steamship, railroad and automobile, a new form of transportation became widespread after World War II. The first airline in the state started in St. Petersburg in 1914 connecting the city with Tampa, a short flight across Tampa Bay. At the time, there were no bridges connecting the city, and reaching Tampa was a long ordeal over miserable roads.

During World War I, Florida was the perfect place for flying and training pilots. The warm, sunny weather allowed year-round flying and attracted airlines to Florida. Pan American began connecting Key West with Havana in 1927. Eastern Airlines began flights to Miami in the 1930s, and National Airlines (founded in St. Petersburg) launched nonstop flights from Miami to New York in 1946. In Henry Flagler's day, the trip from New York to Florida took days; now, it took a few hours.

The airplane's arrival had a dramatic impact on tourism, although Walt Disney never considered the Orlando airport in selecting his site for Disney World.

As the railroads had done decades earlier, the airlines offered package deals combining transportation, airfare and tickets to attractions.

World War II also led to the postwar baby boom and changed Florida's tourism landscape. The early attractions were aimed at adults, whether it was the springs or the beaches. There were no appeals to bring the children.

Between 1946 and 1954, more than thirty major attractions opened, along with scores of smaller ones. The number of tourists soared, going from 2.2 million in 1940 to 10.5 million in 1960. Most of the new attractions were aimed at families, including children.

In the 1950s, Anheuser-Busch saw a major competitor, Schlitz, open a brewery in Tampa, so it opened its own brewery there. Adolphus Busch made a fortune in beer, purchased a magnificent home in Pasadena and built magnificent gardens. He was so proud of them that he opened them to the public.

In 1964, the company built a hospitality center with a small garden and bird show at its Tampa brewery. He added a Swiss House Restaurant and then began expanding with a monorail and wild animals. Visitors got a tour of the brewery—and a free sample of beer—and watched the animals. Anheuser-Busch moved the gardens into a separate division, and Busch Gardens was born.

By accident, Fort Lauderdale created a new attraction: spring break. In the 1930s, students came to Fort Lauderdale for a national swimming competition and stayed to enjoy the beach. In 1960, the movie *Where the Boys Are* showed Yvette Mimieux, Jim Hutton and George Hamilton frolicking on the beach. Connie Francis recorded the hit song from the show, and millions of college students learned that the action was in Florida.

At first, the Fort Lauderdale merchants were thrilled with the influx, until they found it was a mixed blessing. The students arrived in huge numbers—fifty thousand came to Fort Lauderdale for spring break in 1961—but they didn't spend much money and often created problems. And their presence kept older visitors away, particularly families with more money to spend. Fort Lauderdale began to discourage the students, who moved on to other Florida cities such as Daytona Beach. Those cities soon grew tired of the problems and of the image the students created.

A more serious form of tourism developed at the same time up the Florida coast. In 1961, President John Kennedy pledged to land a man on the moon before the decade was over. The space program drew tourists, particularly on launch days, when highways were packed and VIPs competed for front-row seats. It also allowed parents to label their vacation to Florida as educational.

In 1961, the Florida Hotel Commission found 1,374 hotels, 5,765 motels and 10,200 rooming houses in the state. The same year, *Travel U.S.A.* listed the top two dozen attractions in the nation. Florida's two entries were Marineland and Silver Springs, both fading attractions.

Almost from the day Disneyland opened in California in 1955, Disney officials began to consider another park or even a series of parks. Surveys showed that less than 10 percent of the Disneyland visitors came from east of the Mississippi. Briefly, Disney considered creating a chain such as Six Flags. That idea was quickly rejected, and the search began for a single eastern site.

Walt Disney considered several sites, including Niagara Falls and land outside of New York City and Washington, D.C. He even visited St. Louis while considering an urban site.

He decided a warm-weather site was needed and settled on Florida. The search came down to four sites, including one on the east coast and one on the west coast, along with Ocala and Orlando. He rejected the sites on Florida's coasts, saying he did not want to compete against a free attraction—the beach. That left Ocala and Orlando.

Disney flew into Tampa in 1963 as part of the effort to keep his mission a secret. The next day, he drove to Ocala to look at land. Plans to drive to Orlando were scuttled when he found he needed to return to California. He decided to fly over Orlando instead. As he flew over the point where Interstate 4 intersects with Florida's Turnpike, he said, "That's it."

As Walt Disney was flying over Orlando, one thousand miles away, John Kennedy was assassinated in Dallas.

Walt and his brother Roy began assembling 27,000 acres. Roy was the money man, and when he complained about the large amount of land being acquired, Walt responded, "Don't you wish we had bought 27,000 acres in Anaheim?"

The assumption was that Disney wanted to build another version of Disneyland, but Walt had something else in mind. He had become fascinated with cities and began reading books on urban planning. Disney's dream for Florida was to build the city of the future. Initial plans called for an airport and a nuclear power plant. EPCOT is closer to Disney's dream than the Magic Kingdom.

When Walt died at the end of 1966, there were initial questions about whether the Florida project would continue. Roy took over and said the project would go forward as a larger version of Disneyland. When a Disney executive asked about Walt's idea, Roy snapped, "Walt's dead."

Disney's decision to select a site from an airplane had consequences. When Disney employees got to the site, they found that much of the land was underwater. The park took an extra year to build.

It opened in October 1971, and the impact on the Central Florida economy was immediate. The crowds came in huge numbers, packing hotels for miles around. Visitors stayed in hotels as far away as Daytona Beach and Tampa, which helped the other attractions. In the first year, Cypress

The 1971 opening of Disney World's Magic Kingdom changed tourism in Florida, eliminating dozens of small attractions.

Gardens attendance was up 30 percent, Kennedy Space Center jumped 27 percent and Silver Springs increased by 30 percent.

On the day Disney World opened, the owner of Cypress Gardens, Dick Pope, took out a full-page newspaper advertisement welcoming Disney to Florida, and Roy Disney gave him the first lifetime pass to the Magic Kingdom. Pope predicted that Disney World would increase attendance at Cypress Gardens and said, "Anyone who is going to spend $100 million near me is good, and a good thing."

It did not last. As Orlando rushed to build hotel rooms, there was no need to stay outside Orlando. Attendance at other attractions, particularly Cypress Gardens, declined.

The demand for thousands of new hotel rooms set off a construction boom. As one observer noted, everyone decided to build hotel rooms at the same time. When the oil embargo hit in 1973, gas prices soared and visitors stopped coming. Suddenly, there were too many hotel rooms in Orlando, and hundreds of construction workers were out of jobs.

The gasoline shortage led to attractions closing throughout the state. Between 1973 and 1978, twenty venues closed, including Masterpiece Gardens (The Great Masterpiece), McKee Jungle Gardens, Rainbow

Walt Disney and his brother Roy joined Governor Haydon Burns in Orlando to announce plans for Disney's Florida attraction.

Springs and the Aquatarium. In the 1980s, the death toll included Miami Serpentarium, Circus Hall of Fame, Homosassa Springs and Tiki Gardens in Indian Shores.

The gas shortage led to nearly a dozen planned attractions being canceled. The biggest problem for the attractions was not the gas shortage but Disney. Of the 130 major roadside attractions opened from 1929 to the opening of Disney World, just two dozen were still operating in 1998.

Another factor contributing to the decline was the soaring value of land prices. Miami's Rare Bird Farm became a shopping center, and Africa U.S.A. in Boca Raton is now the Camino Gardens subdivision. Others gave way to progress as expressways cut through some attractions such as Musa Isle and Tropical Hobbyland. Some, such as Rainbow Tropical Gardens in Boynton Beach and James Melton's Autorama in Hypoluxo, were on the water and gave way to expensive condos.

The original idea for SeaWorld was an underwater restaurant near San Diego. In 1964, it became the first SeaWorld, followed by one in Cleveland.

Like scores of Florida attractions, Tiki Gardens started small as a gift shop, then added more land and eventually monkeys and a restaurant. The county purchased the land and built a parking lot.

In 1971, as Disney World prepared to open, SeaWorld purchased 125 acres for an Orlando location. It proved a worthy addition to Disney and survived when others faltered. During its first year, it drew 1.7 million visitors, and within a decade, attendance had doubled.

In 1976, Universal's offer to buy SeaWorld was rejected by William Jovanovich, the free-spending president of Harcourt Brace Jovanovich (HBJ),

Miami's Tropical Hobbyland featured Seminole Indians making and selling crafts and wrestling alligators.

Rainbow Tropical Gardens in Boynton Beach was replaced by expensive condos.

the huge publishing company. When Jovanovich led HBJ into a mountain of debt, he was forced out, and SeaWorld, along with Cypress Gardens and Boardwalk and Baseball, were sold to Anheuser-Busch in 1989.

In 2009, Busch sold its amusement parks, including Busch Gardens and SeaWorld, for $2.7 billion.

From the moment Disney announced its plans, there was speculation about other Hollywood studios coming to Florida. Speculation centered on Universal Studios, which had turned its Hollywood Studios into a popular attraction with a studio tour in 1964. Universal kept delaying entering Orlando.

Finally, in 1981, Universal Studios purchased 423 acres on Interstate 4 between SeaWorld and Disney. If Universal had acted sooner, it would have been able to acquire more land. Universal Studios opened in 1990 and began planning for a second park, Islands of Adventure, which opened in 1999. After building two parks and a series of hotels, Universal ran out of room and purchased Wet 'n Wild to tear it down and build a giant hotel.

The arrival of Disney also brought about what became known as the overflow theory. The idea was simple: visitors might spend a day or two, even three, at the Magic Kingdom, but if they had come for a week, that left open days. Perhaps they would spend a couple of days at the beach, or a day at the Kennedy Space Center, SeaWorld or Cypress Gardens.

Even smaller attractions would benefit from the overflow. Visitors might spend only a few days at the Magic Kingdom, but they would leave most of their money there, paying for parking, admission, food and souvenirs. So they might look for less-expensive attractions such as Gatorland.

The overflow theory might have worked, but Disney was not through building, and Universal Studios had not yet opened. In 1975, the Southern Governors' Conference met at Walt Disney World, and Disney used the forum to announce plans for its "experimental prototype community of tomorrow," or EPCOT. The Magic Kingdom was perfect for families with children, but what about older visitors? EPCOT was for them. It opened in 1982 with its huge geodesic sphere dominating the park.

Disney had seen its attendance decline for four years before the EPCOT opening, but that venue sent attendance soaring 81 percent in its first year. Governor Reubin Askew's prediction that EPCOT would bring world peace was off the mark, and the idea that many nations would flock to open pavilions never happened. Still, the park was a success.

Walt Disney once said that it was necessary "to keep the show on the road," by which he meant to keep it up to date. Rides could get old, technology

Universal Studios helped draw more tourists to Florida with its movie-themed rides and roller coasters.

could make for better rides and tastes would change. So the additions to Disney kept coming. Orange County opened a massive convention center in 1983, but Disney responded with its own convention center and opened Typhoon Lagoon water park, Pleasure Island for shopping and nightlife and finally, in 1989, a third park, Disney-MGM Studios.

MGM was a fading studio with the rights to scores of classic movies Disney wanted for the park. The original plan was for the park to be much like Universal Studios Hollywood, a combination movie studio and attraction, but little came of the moviemaking.

In 1995, Disney announced plans for Disney's Wild Animal Kingdom, which opened three years later.

One of Disney's best decisions involved a fleet of buses. At one point, Disney had invited competitors such as SeaWorld and Cypress Gardens to its briefings on new additions to its parks, but gradually it wanted visitors to spend their entire vacation on Disney property. They could board a Disney bus at Orlando International Airport and never set foot outside Disney's twenty-seven thousand acres. When the visitors' vacation was over, the bus would return them to the airport. The buses took them from park to park, then to Disney Springs (the replacement for Paradise Island) or Lake Buena Vista.

To the west, Busch Gardens thrived by adding some of the world's most exciting roller coasters.

With the opening of Disney World, visitors no longer came to Florida, they came to an attraction. People could fly into Orlando International Airport and never come within a dozen miles of the city. It meant they were bypassing scores of smaller attractions, putting them out of business.

The best example was US 27, home of the Bok Tower and two dozen other attractions. One by one, these venues shut their doors, leaving only the Bok Tower as a tourist attraction.

8

THE PANHANDLE ATTRACTIONS

While the Florida peninsula was being developed by millionaires Henry Plant and Henry Flagler, few visitors came to the Panhandle stretching from Tallahassee to Pensacola.

At one time, Florida's Panhandle was twice as large as it is today, until other states began nibbling away. Georgia was the first to take a hunk, pushing the northern border close to Jacksonville. Alabama, Mississippi and Louisiana came next, taking cities from Mobile to Baton Rouge.

What was left was more interested in industry than tourism. In the 1830s, one of the first sawmills in Florida was built in Pensacola. With the introduction of steam engines in the 1840s, production improved, and the amount of lumber doubled, then redoubled.

In 1888, Chicago investors purchased 122,000 acres for as little as twenty-five cents an acre, and the industry came to be dominated by large lumber companies. Turpentine production also became a major industry, used for shipbuilding.

The port at Pensacola offered advantages for shipbuilding and a naval station. In 1825, President John Quincy Adams approved Pensacola for a naval base, and in 1913, the U.S. Navy established a naval air station to train pilots.

In 1929, a new bridge opened Panama City Beach to Panama City and developer Gideon Thomas began developing the 100 acres he owned on the beach. In 1935, J.E. Churchwell took his life savings, purchased 160 acres of beachfront land and founded Long Beach Resort. Both men were roundly ridiculed. It was the middle of the Great Depression, and most thought the men were wasting their money.

Churchwell built accommodations and, slowly, the tourists began coming. By the start of World War II, temporary rides were popular on Long Beach, although they stayed only for the summer months. When winter came, there was only an empty lot. The war brought thousands of sailors and pilots to Pensacola, and when they were not training, they were at the beaches.

After World War II, Churchwell went to California to look at tourist attractions. He met Walt Disney, who was planning an amusement park for Southern California.

He returned and opened a roller rink and a dance floor and installed playground equipment. It was a start, and when rock 'n' roll arrived, the dance floor became a popular hangout.

In 1952, journalist Claude Jenkins coined the phrase "Miracle Strip" to apply to the beaches of Okaloosa Island to the west of Long Beach Resort, and it came to be applied to all the beaches along a 130-mile stretch from Pensacola to Panama City.

It was the civil rights movement that brought permanent rides to the beach. Birmingham, Alabama, became the center of resistance to civil rights, and in 1962, the city closed parks, including Kiddieland, an amusement park operating during the summer.

The rides were moved to Panama City Beach, where Jimmy Lark had hired one of the nation's leading roller-coaster builders to erect the giant wood coaster. It was the start of the Miracle Strip Amusement Park.

In 1950, promotion began for the beaches as efforts were started to extend the tourist season from a few months to year-round.

The attractions began to multiply. Lee Kopplin, the creator of Goofy Golf, opened a course in 1961, and soon there were courses everywhere: Zoo-Land Golf in 1960, Beacon Golf in 1961 and Pirates Cove Golf in 1972.

Koplin found success and decided to build a Western town called Tombstone Territory. It was the name of a television show—one of nearly three dozen Westerns dominating the new medium. There was an Indian trading post with Native American dancers and cliff dwellers, cattle and a totem pole. Visitors traveled in a miniature train called the Iron Horse (named after another television show) to the town with its daily gunfights, bank robbers and refreshments at the saloon. When the shooting stopped, Digger the Undertaker was called in to carry the bodies away.

The Churchwell family saw the success of Tombstone Territory and responded with Petticoat Junction, named after another television program. The show had nothing to do with the West, and the attraction had nothing to do with *Petticoat Junction*, but Churchwell knew one of the show's stars, Edgar Buchanan. It had a regular-sized train called the Cannonball, the same name as the train in the show, that ran in a large circle.

Petticoat Junction added a roller coaster from Oklahoma City and a giant pirate that had previously been a Santa Claus. While the television show ended in 1970, the attraction hung on until 1984.

Other attractions followed, including a two-hundred-foot-tall observation tower that opened in 1966. Nearby was Dracula's Castle on Panama City Beach, with the slogan, "We'll be lurking for you." Long Beach had a deer ranch with a petting zoo.

In 1963, Ross Allen opened a branch of his Silver Springs show in Panama City. Ross Allen's Jungle Show ran for two years before Allen sold it, and the new owners renamed it Seminole Reptile Jungle. A volcano was added, but the park failed, and it became Alvin's Magic Mountain Mall. Alvin kept the volcano, which became the magic mountain. By 2020, the structure was no longer stable and was demolished.

Two things were working against the attractions along the Miracle Strip. The first was the weather. From 1918 to 1974, no big hurricane struck the coast. In 1975, Hurricane Eloise hit the strip with 135-mile-an-hour winds. The devastation was so great that the name *Eloise* was retired from the hurricane name list. It destroyed or damaged hundreds of buildings across the area and caused severe damage at Long Beach Resort. It spelled the end for Tombstone Territory, which closed by the end of the decade.

Hurricane Opal struck twenty years later, causing $2.1 billion in damage. The property values along the coast were increasing dramatically. And the damage caused by the twin hurricanes gave property owners the chance to replace small mom-and-pop motels and attractions with expensive condominiums. No longer were people calling it the "Redneck Riviera." Instead, it was home to million-dollar condos and exclusive communities such as Seaside.

9

CYPRESS GARDENS

As the economy improved in the 1930s, tourists began returning to Florida. While many of the minor attractions disappeared during the worst of the economic downturn, scores survived. The state had beaches, warm weather and several animal shows, but it lacked a destination attraction. It did not have a Niagara Falls or a Grand Canyon, a site people long to visit.

Dick Pope changed that.

The center of Dick Pope's world was Winter Haven, a small town in Central Florida that profited from the boom of the 1920s. The boom led to a road-building program to accommodate the tourists coming to the new Bok Tower to the south.

The boom drew Dick Pope's father from Iowa with the hope of making a fortune in real estate. Dick Pope joined his father's real estate firm and watched as the grand Haven Hotel soared six stories and a country club opened to serve the visitors.

Dick Pope got married, and his future seemed secure: golf with prospective land buyers, membership in the fledgling yacht club and a stream of buyers anxious to get in on the land boom.

Within months of the Pope family's arrival, the boom turned to a bust, and the Pope real estate empire began to crumble. Dick Pope needed a job, and he found the perfect opening, promoting the Johnson Motors outboard division. Pope was able to combine his two passions, waterskiing and promotion.

Cypress Gardens reigned as Florida's premier attraction for more than three decades until Disney arrived.

Pope was an early promoter of waterskiing, creating some of the stunts that became standard at Cypress Gardens. He was the first to sail over obstacles in a speedboat, and he staged stunt shows for Johnson throughout Florida.

His success led him to open his own public relations business. Clients included the Outboard Motorboat Association. For a time, business flourished, but the economic downturn that threw him out of work in Florida spread to the rest of the country, and by 1931, he was once again out of work.

Cypress Gardens installed the Island in the Sky in an unsuccessful effort to draw more tourists.

His wife, Julie, read a magazine article about a businessman in Charleston, South Carolina, who had opened his gardens to the public. The public responded, and the owner took in $36,000 in the first year—a princely sum in the Great Depression.

Pope manufactured orange crates to raise the money to buy sixteen acres near Winter Haven. Lake Eloise had been home to the local yacht club during the booming 1920s, but the boats were gone. He enlisted the help of the Winter Haven Canal Commission to help clear the land and build gardens. He also received support from the federal government, which provided laborers as part of a New Deal program.

His project was dismissed as a dream financed with public dollars. He stopped using public money and agreed to reimburse the canal commission. He was strapped for funds, but his project was now entirely private.

The construction took two years, and the attraction opened in 1935 with the governor on hand. His timing was perfect; tourism was rebounding. The *New Republic* wrote, "The tourist tide is coming in again."

Still, there were other gardens in the state—Highlands Hammock in Sebring and Ravine Gardens in Palatka. Pope needed all his skills as a promoter to make Cypress Gardens stand out.

He survived until 1940, when a winter freeze turned out to be a blessing. Many of the flowers were killed, and Julie Pope worried that the crowds would stop coming. She decided to dress the attraction's female employees in old-fashioned hoopskirt dresses. They became the symbol for the attraction, and attendance increased.

Dick Pope went off to war after Pearl Harbor, and Julie took over sole management. Gasoline rationing meant a decline in tourism, and she worked to attract servicemen stationed in Central Florida. When a local newspaper ran a picture of women skiing at Cypress Gardens, servicemen turned up saying they wanted to see them. Julie quickly assembled a group of women to put on a waterskiing show without preparation.

The servicemen returned to their bases with stories about the beautiful women, and soldiers began arriving by the busload.

By accident, waterskiing became the trademark of the gardens, and the women began appearing on magazine covers. In 1947, barefoot waterskiing began, drawing national attention.

The gardens became the backdrop for a series of movies, including *On an Island with You* starring Esther Williams and Peter Lawford, *Easy to Love* with Williams and Van Johnson and Frank Capra's *A Hole in the Head* with Frank Sinatra.

Cypress Gardens boomed during the 1950s.

Pope and Walt Disney had been friends for years, and Disney sought Pope's advice in developing Disneyland in the 1950s.

The year Walt Disney picked Orlando as the site for his new theme park, Cypress Gardens and the Grand Canyon were tied as the top tourist destinations in the United States. And US 27 was still a major highway delivering tourists on their way to Miami on Pope's doorstep.

When Disney announced plans to build a park near Orlando, Pope was thrilled. Shortly after the announcement, Pope said, "We welcome Walt Disney and his brother Roy, and all the rest of them with open arms." He did not see it as competition but as another drawing card for Central Florida. Pope took out a full-page advertisement in the *Orlando Sentinel* on the day Disney World opened. "Cypress Gardens Welcomes THE MAGIC KINGDOM OF DISNEY."

Pope received the first lifetime pass to Disney World. On the day Disney opened, the top three attractions in Florida were Cypress Gardens, Bok Tower and Silver Springs.

Pope came from a time when people drove through Florida on their way to a destination. Along the way, they stopped at attractions for brief visits. In a single day, it was possible to visit several US 27 attractions.

In 1972, Disney's first full year, Cypress Gardens' attendance jumped 38 percent. At Cape Kennedy, attendance increased by 27 percent, and Silver Springs saw a 28 percent jump.

Visitors spent one or two days at Disney World, then headed for the nearby attractions or the beach. Attendance peaked in the late 1970s. The numbers were deceiving. Central Florida tourism exploded, and Disney World was forced to close some days. Cypress Gardens was getting a smaller piece of the tourism pie. Still, Pope was optimistic. "It's fantastic. Maybe 60 percent of our visitors go to Disney first.…Our business is up every year. And how can you fail with people who are happy?"

Pope's son Dick Pope Jr. took over operating the park, and there were half-hearted attempts to appeal to younger tourists. There was the Wacky Water Park, the Swamper Stomper and the Castle Bounce House, but nothing worked.

In 1985, the Pope family sold out to the giant publishing company Harcourt Brace Jovanovich (HBJ), which was building an attractions empire. The family received $23 million. William Jovanovich—who had added his name to the venerable firm—came under financial pressure. After just four years and a huge financial investment, he sold all the HBJ attractions—SeaWorld, Cypress Gardens and the struggling Boardwalk and Baseball—to Busch Entertainment Corporation. Busch worked hard to draw more visitors, adding shops and attractions.

The Busch magic failed at Cypress Gardens, and in 1995, Busch sold out—"unloaded" might be a better term—to the park's management. In 1999, a paddle-wheel boat and an extreme ski show were added. They were just small additions, overshadowed by Disney, SeaWorld and Universal to the east and Busch Gardens to the west. The new petting zoo and a used roller coaster from Panama City could not compete with Space Mountain. Attendance continued to fall, and the new owners lacked the financial strength to make a massive overhaul.

The park closed in 2003; employees received just three days' notice. Six months later, the park was sold again and renamed Cypress Gardens Adventure Park. The deal included selling off 150 acres to a trust to conserve land. The new owners were left with a small part of the original Pope land.

The park reopened just as four hurricanes slammed the state, three of which hurt Cypress Gardens. Any hope of rebirth ended, and the owners declared bankruptcy in 2006. It was sold at auction for $16.9 million and reopened in 2009 with a new water park, Splash Island. The rides were gone, along with the animals. Within months, the buyers gave up, closing the park on a moment's notice.

After nearly seventy-five years, Dick Pope's dream died. A long list of operators tried and failed to keep it going. The death ushered in a new park, Legoland.

On January 15, 2010, Merlin Entertainments purchased what remained of Cypress Gardens for its fifth Legoland. After extensive remodeling, the park opened in October 2011.

Legoland salvaged some Cypress Gardens rides, although they were renamed. The ski shows remain, along with many of the plants and flowers. In 2018, Dick Pope's most prominent attraction, Island in the Sky, was closed. It had opened in 1983 as one of the many attempts to infuse new life into the park. Island in the sky lifted visitors 150 feet into the air while a circular platform revolved. Legoland tried to keep it going, but there were constant mechanical problems, and the ride closed in 2017.

The first Legoland opened in Denmark in 1968, and thirty years later, another opened in California. When Disney World opened, Merlin executives were bombarded with the "When are you coming to Florida?" question.

As EPCOT opened a decade later, it appeared as though the question would be answered. Disney proposed a Denmark pavilion that would feature a recreation of the Tivoli Gardens. A Lego boat ride would sail among the gardens, which would feature Danish landmarks—built from Legos, of course.

The talks continued until 1983, and Disney believed that a deal was so close that it went ahead and built the bathrooms for the attraction. Disney also proposed a section of Disney World dedicated to Legos, but nothing came of the talks.

10

CIRCUS WORLD

N o Florida attraction had more lives than what began as Circus World west of Orlando and about twenty miles from Disney World. It was one of the attractions created in the wake of Walt Disney's decision to come to Florida.

For half a century, the winter headquarters of the Ringling Bros. and Barnum & Bailey Circus was in Sarasota. The owners decided to create a Florida attraction to combine the winter headquarters, the well-known Clown College and a theme park for visitors.

The plans were announced with great fanfare in 1972, a year after the opening of Disney World. The initial plans included a nineteen-story, elephant-shaped hotel and a residential community. The community was to be called Barnum City. Those never happened, as the park moved from owner to owner and theme to theme. Parts of the attraction opened in 1974.

Irvin Feld, who owned the circus, sold out to Mattel as construction began, and in 1973, Mattel placed the park and the circus up for sale. A subsidiary of Gulf Oil agreed to purchase the circus in 1974, and the opening of the park was pushed back. Gulf Oil changed its mind and backed out and then reopened the negotiations. Once again, the opening was pushed back, to 1976.

When it finally did open, the results were encouraging. Attendance peaked at 1.3 million in 1979, and the park turned a profit in 1980. But 1979 was the peak, as attendance declined for the next five years.

Circus World began with ambitious plans, but constant changes in ownership and theme doomed the attraction.

Feld repurchased the circus from Mattel in 1982, but the toy company kept Circus World and added shows, rides and a new roller coaster. It didn't help.

The problems became critical in 1982 with the opening of EPCOT. When Disney's only attraction was the Magic Kingdom, visitors spending a week were left with several days to visit other parks. Once EPCOT opened, visitors had less time for other attractions and had to choose between SeaWorld, Busch Gardens in Tampa, Cypress Gardens, the nearby beaches and the Kennedy Space Center.

Jim Monaghan bought the park in 1983 and added nine major thrill rides and six youth rides.

In 1985, as Monaghan deemphasized the circus part of his attraction, he auctioned off some of the park's holdings, including an original 1921 Coney Island carousel. The park made a profit in 1985, but Monaghan saw the problems ahead and wanted out.

He found a willing buyer in Harcourt Brace Jovanovich in 1986. William Jovanovich had assumed control of the publishing firm Harcourt Brace and

In an ill-fated attempt to reinvent itself, Circus World became Boardwalk and Baseball.

began to diversify. He snapped up SeaWorld and Cypress Gardens during his buying spree. Without notice, he shut down Circus World and ordered it rebuilt as Boardwalk and Baseball.

Circus World seemed like a good idea, but it was hurt by its location—it was an additional half-hour drive from Disney World. And its old-fashioned theme did not appeal to younger visitors who wanted the Disney experience.

Like Circus World, Boardwalk and Baseball was a throwback to another time, when people walked along the boardwalk of resorts such as Atlantic City.

The park was divided into two parts. The boardwalk section had more than thirty rides, including a giant wooden roller coaster. The baseball part was ambitious: There were artifacts from the National Baseball Hall of Fame, and the Kansas City Royals agreed to make it their spring training site. A couple of minor-league teams also agreed to play there. HBJ spent $50 million transforming the park and adding the stadium.

Even at the grand opening in 1987, industry observers predicted failure. The three HBJ parks offered a combination ticket, and attendance at Boardwalk and Baseball was 1.35 million in 1988 but dropped to 1.0 million the following year. There were extensive layoffs and a reduction in hours. Guests complained that the park was dirty.

Cypress Gardens was doing even worse, and HBJ wanted out of the theme-park business. SeaWorld and Cypress Gardens were sold to Busch Entertainment in 1989, and Boardwalk and Baseball was shut down in 1990. The shutdown came so quickly that there were still visitors on rides when the park closed.

The park was torn down, except for the stadium and an IMAX theater. The baseball teams drifted away, and eventually, the stadium and the theater were torn down. Today, the site is a shopping center.

11

THE NEVER WERE ATTRACTIONS

uthor Diane Roberts called Florida the "Dream State," and millions of people brought their dreams to the state. Many came with plans to open an attraction. Seeing others succeed, they believed they could find their fortune in the sun. Many thought they could profit from the coming of Disney. If an attraction could pick off just a small percentage of the Disney visitors, money could be made.

Dozens of promoters ended with little more than newspaper clippings announcing their grand plans. For every attraction that became a reality, a dozen never got beyond the planning stage.

In the late 1950s, a group of developers planned to build Paris USA on 150 acres near the Dade County–Broward County line. There would be a one-thousand-foot replica of the Eiffel Tower, and the developers predicted it would soon draw two million visitors a year. Despite promises that the park would open in 1959, work never began.

Soon after Walt Disney announced his plans, Western star Roy Rogers appeared at a press conference with Governor Haydon Burns to announce plans for a giant resort and dude ranch. The project died quietly, as Roy and his wife, Dale Evans, retired from show business and opened a museum near his Apple Valley, California home. It later moved to Victorville, then to Branson, Missouri. It closed in 2009, and the contents—including a stuffed Trigger and Bullet—were auctioned off.

In the early 1980s, Doug Henning was one of the nation's hottest magicians, with a long-running Broadway show and television specials.

There were even Doug Henning dolls. In the mid-1980s, he retired from the stage and devoted his efforts to Transcendental Meditation. He studied at Maharishi University in Switzerland, and with Maharishi Mahesh Yogi he began drafting plans for a theme park. They started talking about a $1.5 billion attraction called Veda Land at Niagara Falls. It would include a building suspended above the water. Nothing ever came of that project, and Henning became a serial announcer for his theme parks. He always drew a lot of publicity. In 1990, he announced plans to build the park in Kissimmee, not far from Disney's Main Gate. He said the park would open in 1993 and "reach people on a deeper level, to stimulate their intellect, arouse their emotions and touch their inner human consciousness." In 1998, the *New York Times* ran a story headlined "Veda Lost" about Henning's failed plans. Henning died in 2000 of liver cancer, and Veda Land came to an end.

In 1994, singer Charlie Daniels, best known for his hit "The Devil Went Down to Georgia," was in Las Vegas attending a rodeo when he and a stockbroker came up with an idea for a rodeo arena in Pasco County, Florida, north of Tampa. The more Daniels talked about the project, the bigger it became: concert venues, hotels, golf courses and a Western theme park built on 1,954 acres. There would even be a 3D show based on his hit record. Design firms were hired, and a 1997 opening date was announced. All that was missing was financing, which never materialized.

In 2005, plans were announced for Paidia's DestiNations Theme Park and Resort. It was to be built on 140 acres near Disney's Main Gate—the land once to be home to Doug Henning's Veda Land—and had a construction budget of $300 million. The backers issued a vague press release promising, "We seek to bring the world's most exotic and exciting places together and put them within reach, and at the very heart and essence of our mission in the quest for peace and hope." It was never heard from again.

In 2010, an investor group announced the Orlando Thrill Park to be built on International Drive in Orlando. The attraction was to feature several roller coasters and other rides on seventy acres. The investors had the money, the ability and the plans but quickly ran into opposition from neighbors in the Tangelo Park neighborhood. After a year, the City of Orlando denied approval, and the plan died.

At one time, a stop at the local Blockbuster was as normal as stopping at the grocery store or gas station. At its height, there were nine thousand Blockbuster stores. The company was the creation of Wayne Huizenga. As Blockbuster peaked, Huizenga came up with Blockbuster Park—which jokesters called Wayne's World. It would be a sprawling sport and theme park in South Florida. Huizenga had elaborate plans drawn up and submitted them to local officials and the Florida legislature. As the project moved toward approval, he sold the entire company to Viacom, the entertainment conglomerate, which had no interest in his park and immediately killed the plan. Viacom owned Paramount, which already had its own theme parks. This led to repeated rumors that the company was going to move into Florida. Paramount-owned parks included Kings Island in Ohio, Kings Dominion in Virginia, Carowinds in North Carolina and Great America in California. As Disney and Universal announced plans to open movie-themed attractions, it seemed only natural that Paramount would join the list. There were only rumors, and Viacom wanted to get out of the theme park business, not increase its holdings. Eventually, the parks were sold to Cedar Fair.

Interama was to be a permanent international exposition in Miami. It would highlight culture, trade and education and be a combination business center and amusement park. The idea dates to 1919, when Miami mayor Everest Sewell first proposed a Pan-American trade mart. In 1939, the Florida State Chamber of Commerce passed a resolution calling for a trade mart in Miami. In 1950, the federal government approved a government-sponsored Inter-American Center in Miami, and several Latin American republics soon signed on. The following year, the state created the Inter-American Authority and a 1,600-acre site north of central Miami that had once been the site of a planned airport. Elaborate plans were drawn up; there was to be a spire and hanging gardens. Planning went on for a decade as plans were made, then abandoned. In 1964, construction began, and July 4, 1968, was set as the opening date. Construction was so slow that by the opening date, little had been done. As the 1976 bicentennial grew closer, Miami was a possible site for celebrations. Interama went through its third revision, this time to highlight the history of the United States. By 1974, just one building was completed, and President Gerald Ford canceled funds for further development. The project finally died, and the City of North Miami was stuck with bond payments. The state stepped in and bailed out North Miami by purchasing part of the land for the Bay Vista campus for Florida International University.

Louis Cartier made a fortune in British grocery stores. In the 1980s, he purchased 1,328 acres near Disney World with plans to build an English village. Cartier cleared the land and started construction on a few buildings. Although a preview center opened, a host of problems developed. The most serious was financial. While Cartier was wealthy, his plan included

Miami's Interama took nearly sixty years to finally die. It started in 1919 as a proposal for a Pan-American trade mart. In 1950, it finally received approval, and nearly a quarter of a century later, construction began. But just one building was finished before it was finally killed in 1976.

importing all the materials from England to build an authentic British town. The second problem was with the materials themselves. The British oak had worked well in England but provided a feast for Florida insects and withered in the Florida humidity. Everything had to be torn down, and the land was used for hotels, gift shops and a housing development.

There were dozens of other plans, including David Copperfield's Underground, which was originally planned as an attraction at Disney World; Hurricane World; Winter Wonderland; and Bible World. Johnny Weissmuller pushed Johnny Weissmuller's Tropical Wonderland in Titusville, which was a memory by 1973.

12

DISNEY ATTRACTIONS

Disney has had its share of canceled projects.

Disney's Grand Floridian Resort & Spa is the grandest of the Disney hotels, but the site was originally planned for Disney's Asian Resort, a Thai-themed venue. The Venetian Resort was to be an Italian-themed attraction near the Contemporary Resort. Other canceled hotels were the Persian Resort and the Mediterranean Resort.

In the Magic Kingdom, plans for the Enchanted Snow Palace inside Fantasyland never materialized. It was to be an indoor boat ride inspired by the Snow Queen story. It included the Northern Lights, fairies and polar bears. Disney thought the park needed more thrill rides, and the Snow Queen ride was shelved.

There was almost an additional land in the Magic Kingdom. Shadowlands would have been behind Tomorrowland and feature all the Disney villains. The centerpiece would have been Bald Mountain from "Night on Bald Mountain" from *Fantasia*. A ride would take visitors past the threatening villains.

Pirates of the Caribbean is one of the best-known rides at Disney World, but originally, Disney planned a different water ride featuring a Wild West theme. Western River Expedition would have taken visitors down the Mississippi, and they would have encountered buffalo, stagecoaches and robbers. Instead, Splash Mountain and Big Thunder Mountain are on the site.

In 2001, Disney released the movie *Atlantis: The Lost Empire*. The company had high hopes for the film and planned a Fire Mountain ride. The movie did not do as well as anticipated at the box office, tourism declined after the 9/11 terror attacks and the ride was canceled.

EPCOT has also had its share of canceled projects. The original concept for EPCOT was that it would be a kind of permanent world's fair, with many nations represented. In the end, only a handful of pavilions were built, but initially, there were hopes that dozens of countries would build pavilions.

The Costa Rican Pavilion was to have a large greenhouse filled with tropical plants and birds. The Equatorian African Pavilion would have a sixty-foot treehouse with a live show called *Heartbeat of Africa*.

Disney was so sure that there would be an Israeli Pavilion that billboards advertised it. The plan to re-create ancient Jerusalem ran into budget problems and political reality. There were security concerns as real-world politics came to EPCOT. The Iranian Pavilion also fell victim to reality. It was to have featured a ride through Persian history and a shopping bazaar. Any thought of an Iranian Pavilion ended when the Shah of Iran was overthrown in the Iranian Revolution. Likewise, the United Arab Emirates Pavilion was to contain a magic carpet ride through the history of the contributions of the Middle East to science.

Another "sure thing" for EPCOT was a Soviet Union Pavilion in EPCOT's phase two, featuring a replica of St. Basil's Cathedral. As with Iran and Israel, the real world intervened, and the project came to a screeching halt with the collapse of the Soviet Union.

Plans for the Venezuela Pavilion were to have included an aerial tram ride. The Spanish Pavilion, advertised on billboards in the mid-1980s, also never happened. Nothing came of the plan to build a Switzerland Pavilion with a Matterhorn bobsled ride.

The Japanese Pavilion was to include a movie about Japan's history. The Japanese wanted to leave out World War II, which could anger American veterans. A building for the movie was built but not used, and plans for a Mount Fuji roller coaster were also scuttled. Mount Fuji would tower above the park, and the ride would take passengers inside and outside the mountain. Another idea was the Godzilla Bullet Train Ride, with passengers being threatened by Godzilla. The idea for the ride was transferred to Expedition Everest in Animal Kingdom.

Disney also hoped for a German pavilion and planned a Rhine River Cruise. Boats would take riders through the Black Forest, Oktoberfest and the Cologne Cathedral.

A Thames River Cruise was planned as part of the United Kingdom Pavilion, with guests sailing by the Tower of London and the Houses of Parliament.

IllumiNations: Reflections of Earth was an EPCOT stalwart, a giant fireworks show at the end of the day. After nearly twenty years, the show ended in 2019.

Tapestry of Nations was a parade designed to mark the turn of the century. It opened in 1999 and closed in 2001, although it continued as Tapestry of Dreams for two more years.

Kitchen Kabaret was one of the opening attractions at EPCOT and ran for a dozen years before becoming Food Rocks for another decade. It featured animatronic food signage about good nutrition. Food Rocks was updated with characters including Food Wrapper (Get it? "Rapper"?), the Refrigerator Police (The Police) and the Peach Boys (Beach Boys). The building housing the attraction was torn down to make way for Soarin'.

Wonders of Life ran from 1989 to 2007 with a ride best known for upsetting stomachs. And there was the short-lived Magical World of Barbie, which ran for just two years in the mid-1990s in the American Gardens Theater. The song-and-dance show featured Barbie and Ken, along with lots of costumes and vehicles.

Plans for Disney's Hollywood Studios originally included a Roger Rabbit attraction with a flight simulator. The plan called for a trolley ride taking guests to Maroon Studios, where the Rock 'n' Roller Coaster Starring Aerosmith is located today. There were legal problems over the rights, and the development was put on hold.

Mickey's Movieland was to have a replica of Walt's original Hyperion Avenue Studio, with visitors seeing how the movies were made in the early days. Some elements of the plan ended up in the Magic of Disney Animation. The death of Muppet creator Jim Henson ended plans for the Muppet Studios around 1990. Only Muppet Vision 3D was finished before everything stopped. The Great Movie Ride opened with Disney-MGM Studios in 1989, housed in a replica of Grauman's Chinese Theatre. It closed in 2017.

Following Warren Beatty's Dick Tracy movie, Disney announced a Dick Tracy's Crime Stoppers ride to take visitors through the streets of 1920s Chicago. Disney hoped the movie would lead to sequels and running popularity. The movie did not do as well as expected, and plans for a movie franchise and a Disney attraction were dropped.

Perhaps the strangest proposal for Disney Studios was for the Creatures' Choice Awards. It was to be an animatronic show to honor monsters. Godzilla was to be the guest of honor.

Planners for Animal Kingdom originally envisioned the addition of the Beastly Kingdom. It would feature mythical creatures such as dragons and unicorns. There was to be a giant walk-through maze called Quest of the Unicorn. Ironically, while Disney did not go through with the plans, laid-off Disney employees took the idea to Universal, where it became the Flying Unicorn. There was also to be a boat ride called Fantasia Gardens and a roller coaster to take visitors through a land inhabited by dangerous dragons. Fantastic Gardens did become a miniature golf course.

In its entire history, Disney has had only two parks closed for good, River Country and Discovery Island. River Country was the first Disney water park, opening in 1976. It utilized water from nearby Bay Lake and became an immediate hit. It was supposed to be like an old-fashioned swimming hole with a sandy bottom and untreated water. The lake water created a problem. An eleven-year-old boy died after contracting an amoebic brain infection in 1980. Two other children drowned. In 1989, Disney opened a second water park, Typhoon Lagoon, which had better parking and more amenities. In 1995, it opened Blizzard Beach. Disney closed River Country in 2001 with the expectation that it would reopen in the spring of 2002. As the expected opening date approached, Disney announced that the park would only reopen if there was enough guest demand. That never happened. Four years later, Disney announced the permanent closing of the park. The site sat abandoned for seventeen years, rotting and becoming overgrown. While it was fenced off, it did not discourage those who climbed over the fence to explore.

The second major Disney failure was Discovery Island in the Magic Kingdom. Guests began going to the eleven-acre island in 1974 to walk around and see the animals and birds. Twenty-five years later, it closed. At first, it was called Treasure Island and then Discovery Island. Disney charged admission to the island, which was Disney's second attraction to open after the Magic Kingdom. The animals included monkeys, vultures, toucans, pelicans and alligators. When the attraction closed, many animals were relocated to the new Animal Kingdom.

Since 1999, the island has sat abandoned. The original buildings and attractions are still there, and adventurers have often made their way to the island.

Disney's Main Street Electrical Parade was a crowd favorite that began in 1977 and came to an end in 2016.

Disney's *Captain EO* had everything going for it. The star was Michael Jackson, the script was written by George Lucas and the film was directed by Francis Ford Coppola. The ride opened in 1986 and closed in 1998 amid claims about Jackson and young boys. It was brought back in 2010 after Jackson's death and closed permanently in 2015.

Honey, I Shrunk the Audience opened in 1994, based on the popular movie *Honey, I Shrunk the Kids*. The audience wore 3D glasses and was "shrunk" for the ride by a professor's gadget. Its run was sandwiched between the two Captain EO runs.

EPCOT's Norway Pavilion originally featured a boat ride through Norwegian history, with polar bears and Vikings and even a troll, with some steep rapids thrown in. After twenty-six years, it was replaced by a *Frozen*-themed ride with the stars from that movie.

The Sum of All Thrills was part of the Innoventions section of EPCOT. It opened in 2009, sponsored by Raytheon as part of a program to interest students in math and science. Sum of All Thrills allowed riders to choose their own attraction. They could travel by roller coaster, jet or bobsled. Raytheon's sponsorship ended in 2016, and the ride closed, along with several other Innoventions attractions, including Habit Heroes and StormStruck.

Horizons opened in 1983 as part of EPCOT's Phase 2. It took riders through the future and allowed them to choose their path, traveling to a desert farm or an undersea base. It closed in 1994 after General Electric ended its sponsorship. As General Electric withdrew, the ride began having increased technical problems, breaking down often. When two other attractions closed for refurbishment, Horizons was reopened and operated for four years before being demolished to make room for Mission Space, which opened in 2003.

World of Motion was an original EPCOT ride when the park opened in 1982. It took riders through the history of transportation and was sponsored by General Motors. Guests rode through a series of exhibits, ending with futuristic cars and technology. The ride closed in 1986, because General Motors wanted to sponsor a new ride: Test Track.

Journey into Imagination in EPCOT contained eighty special effects as the ride rotated around a blimp. There were major issues with Kodak's sponsorship, and it closed for revisions in 1998, opening a year later as Journey into YOUR Imagination. Unfortunately, the new ride was a flop. As the complaints mounted, Disney shut it down in 2001. It came back a year later as Journey into Imagination with Figment the Dragon. Kodak's sponsorship ended in 2010, but the ride continues.

The Universe of Energy was an original EPCOT attraction, tracing the history of energy and sponsored by Exxon. It was considered by many to be the most boring ride in EPCOT and was replaced by Ellen's Energy Adventure with Ellen DeGeneres in 1996. Ellen wanted to be on *Jeopardy!*, if only she knew the energy-related questions to the posed answers. Science guy Bill Nye came to her rescue with the questions. It was replaced by the indoor roller coaster Guardians of the Galaxy, which opened in 2022.

The Studio Backlot Tour was an original attraction at Disney Studios, modeled after the very successful tour at Universal Studios in California. It combined a walking tour and a tram ride. At the time, it was thought that Disney would have a working studio. The ride closed in 2014 to make room for Toy Story Lane.

The Great Movie Ride opened in 1989 in Disney's Hollywood Studios and became a popular fixture. Originally planned for EPCOT, it became the centerpiece for Disney Studios. The ride took guests through scenes from movies such as *The Wizard of Oz*, *Raiders of the Lost Ark* and *Mary Poppins*. It finally closed in 2017 to make room for Mickey & Minnie's Runaway Railway.

In front of the Great Movie Ride was the Sorcerer's Hat, which debuted in 2001 as part of 100 Years of Magic to mark Walt Disney's 100th birthday. Inside the hat, visitors could learn about Disney and his work. The displays were removed when the observance ended, and the hat became the venue for the grand opening of Star Tours. The hat was removed in 2015.

While some of Disney World's earliest rides have been replaced, others have been repurposed.

When the Magic Kingdom first opened, the park's official airline was Eastern Airlines, When Eastern filed for bankruptcy, Delta took over. Delta sponsored Delta Dreamflight in Tomorrowland from 1989 to 1998. It taught travelers the history of flight and even included a travel agent available to sell tickets to Delta flights. When Delta ended its sponsorship in 1996, the ride was rebranded without a sponsor until it was replaced by Buzz Lightyear's Space Ranger Spin in 1998.

The Skyway gondola was a staple at Disneyland and became equally popular at Disney World when the park opened in 1971. The swaying gondolas took riders from Fantasyland to Tomorrowland or vice versa, giving riders a great view of the park. The ride could be confusing, as riders assumed the ride would bring them back to the starting point instead of depositing them far away. The ride passed through the Matterhorn, which was used as a support for the monorail. Stress cracks began appearing in the Matterhorn, and there was extensive metal fatigue. In the 1990s, Disney president Michael Eisner cast a critical eye on Disney rides, evaluating how much space each took up and how efficient they were at carrying passengers. The gondola ride could carry only four passengers in each gondola, and it took time to load the gondolas and send them on their way. In 1994, Disneyland closed the ride, and Disney World followed five years later.

The 20,000 Leagues under the Sea was also copied from a Disneyland ride, based on a Disney movie. The 20,000 Leagues under the Sea ride took up a great deal of space, and the submarine had limited room for guests. Plus, it was showing its age and leaks were beginning to appear. Without advance notice, the ride closed in 1994, with a promise that it would reopen in 1996 after maintenance. Shortly before it was to reopen, Disney announced that the ride had closed permanently. The submarines were removed, and most were buried in a landfill.

The lagoon was still there and was renamed Ariel's Grotto until 2004, when the lagoon was drained and the site turned into Pooh's Playful Spot, which lasted until 2010, when it gave way to the Seven Dwarfs Mine Train.

One of the most loved rides was Mr. Toad's Wild Ride, which was copied from a ride at Disneyland. Mr. Toad appears in a little-known Disney movie, *The Adventures of Ichabod and Mr. Toad*. In an old-fashioned car, you rode through a series of disasters.

Eisner's review put Mr. Toad on the chopping block in 1997, but there was pushback from Toad fans, who showed up wearing protest outfits. The protest gave Mr. Toad one more year. The Many Adventures of Winnie the Pooh replaced Mr. Toad, although the track for the ride remained largely the same.

Minnie's Country House in Mickey's Toontown Fair was located between Fantasyland and Tomorrowland. Minnie's Country House was a walk-through attraction featuring photographs of her friends and family and Minnie's taste in furniture. It opened in 1996, replacing Mickey's Hollywood Theater. It closed in 2011 to make way for the expansion of Fantasyland.

Snow White's Adventures in Fantasyland was one of the Magic Kingdom's original rides, but it was too scary for young children. In 1994, it closed for a redesign to make it friendlier. The name was updated to Snow White's Scary Adventures to warn parents what to expect. Still, there were complaints, and it closed for good in 2012.

Mike Fink Keel Boats were first seen in Disney's *Davy Crockett* television program in the 1950s. They were used in Disneyland and were an original ride in Disney World. The boats left from a dock at Liberty Square, then moved to Frontierland, where they ended their run in 2001.

The Flight to the Moon ride took guests to the moon through moving seats and animatronics. It was already outdated when it opened in 1971 in Tomorrowland. Thanks to the Apollo moon landing in 1969, the moon no longer held the mysteries it once did. The ride closed in 1975 to make way for Mission to Mars, which proved to be more futuristic and popular. It closed in 1993 to make room for ExtraTERRORestrial Alien Encounter.

ExtraTERRORestrial Alien Encounter opened in 1995 and lasted eight years. The premise of the show was that an alien research company had an accident and an alien appeared to terrorize the audience. It sprayed a mist on the terrified audience, whose members were locked in their seats and unable to escape. Many thought it was the most frightening ride at Disney World. There were complaints from parents who said it was too frightening for their children. Efforts to make it less scary failed, and it closed in 2003.

It was replaced by the equally scary Stitch's Great Escape. In 2016, the operating dates were cut back, and it was closed permanently in 2018.

Primeval Whirl was a roller coaster in the Animal Kingdom. When it opened in 2002, it was compared unfavorably to the nearby Dinosaur ride and was one of the park's poorest draws. The spinning roller coaster led to complaints of whiplash and nausea. In 2019, its operating days were reduced, and in 2020, it was closed and torn down.

Jessica Rabbit is remembered as the sex symbol of the movie *Who Framed Roger Rabbit*. Disney made several attempts to capitalize on the movie, with no success. Jessica's of Hollywood was a tribute to Jessica in the form of a store at Disney's Pleasure Island. Surprisingly for Disney, it sold lingerie—approved by Jessica. It closed in 1992.

Pleasure Island, a collection of stores, restaurants and entertainment, closed in 2008 to make way for Disney Springs, a collection of stores, restaurants and entertainment.

13

UNIVERSAL ATTRACTIONS

No matter how successful a theme park is, there is a need to make constant changes, update rides, kill outdated attractions and add rides featuring the latest movies. Since Universal Studios Florida opened in 1990, some three dozen attractions have closed.

Within two years of opening, Universal was taking a hard look at attendance figures and closed An American Tail Theatre. It was a live show based on the movie *An American Tail.* There was lots of singing, with the mice trying to get rid of the cats in America, a plot that visitors found lacking. When it closed, Universal opened Fievel's Playland, a playground with large props to make the children feel like mice. Beatlejuice's Rock and Roll Graveyard Revue replaced Fievel and lasted until 2016, although it was changed several times and the name was changed to Beetlejuice's Graveyard Mash-Up. The theater sat empty for two years, then, like Disaster!, became home to Fast & Furious: Supercharged.

Problems for what was considered Universal's premier ride began on opening day in 1990. The Jaws attraction placed guests on tour boats for what was supposed to be a leisurely cruise around Amity Harbor interrupted by shark attacks. From the start, there were huge mechanical difficulties. Parts of the ride had to be rebuilt. The ride was removed in 2012 to clear the area for The Wizarding World of Harry Potter–Diagon Alley.

One of the original attractions was Alfred Hitchcock: The Art of Making Movies, which opened with the park. The attraction featured the shower scene from *Psycho* narrated by Anthony Perkins, who plays Norman Bates. It had a thirteen-year run and was replaced by Shrek 4-D. Shrek and Donkey had to rescue Fiona in a 3D attraction.

The Adventures of Rocky and Bullwinkle Show opened in 1992 and featured a live stage performance with characters from the television show, including Rocky, Bullwinkle, Boris, Natasha, Dudley Do-Right and Snidely Whiplash. It was canceled within a year to make room for StarToons. It ranks as one of the shortest runs at Universal.

Another live-action show was the Wild Wild Wild West Stunt Show, which opened in 1991. It featured cowboys performing stunts and survived until 2003. In 2005, Fear Factor Live, based on the television show, opened and closed in 2020 as the COVID pandemic began. The Funtastic World of Hanna-Barbera was one of the original Universal rides, featuring Yogi, the Flintstones, Scooby-Doo and the Jetsons. It was one of the first rides visitors encountered as they entered the park and ran for a dozen years before giving way to Jimmy Neutron's Nicktoon Blast, which was replaced a decade later by Despicable Me Minion Mayhem.

Earthquake: The Big One opened with the park in 1990, based on the movie of the same name. Visitors traveled a subway train through San Francisco's Embarcadero Station as an earthquake struck. It ran in its original form until 2002, then became home to a series of rides based on other films, including *How the Grinch Stole Christmas* and *E.T.: The Extra-Terrestrial*. In 2008, it became Disaster!, which ran until 2015, when it made way for Fast & Furious: Supercharged.

When the park opened, the television show *Murder, She Wrote* was riding high in the ratings. When the show was canceled in 1996, the attraction was closed. It was a backstage look at how the show was made, including sound effects and video tricks. Next door was the MCA Recording Studio, which closed at the same time. The studio allowed visitors to sing along to songs and purchase a recording of their performance.

Murder, She Wrote, and the MCA Recording Studio were turned into Hercules and Xena: Wizards of the Screen. Stage 54 next door became Donkey's Photo Finish, which featured an animated donkey from *Shrek* greeting visitors. Hercules and Xena were based on two popular television series. Like its predecessor, the attraction was a backstage look at how the shows were made. It lasted only a few years, and the building sat empty for several years before being used for Halloween Horror Nights. In an odd twist, Orange County officials condemned the building. Universal tore it down and built Transformers: The Ride 3D.

In most cases, rides are dropped because they are outdated and drawing smaller crowds, but sometimes, theme parks buy the rights to use a movie for a set number of years. That is what happened with Ghostbusters Spooktacular, which closed in 1996. It was replaced by Twister, based on the movie starring Bill Paxton and Helen Hunt. Visitors experienced a simulated tornado. It lasted for sixteen years before closing in 2015.

The series of *Back to the Future* movies were must-sees, and Universal created a Back to the Future ride. Visitors took seats in a DeLorean with gull-wing doors and sped through history, from the dinosaurs to the future. The ride opened in 1991, a year after the park opened. Passengers in cars went on the search for Biff Tannen. Steven Spielberg, the producer of the films, was a consultant for the ride. Spielberg first brought up the idea of a ride in 1986 after going with George Lucas on a Star Tours ride at Disneyland. With all the movie-themed rides, interest waned. In 2007, the ride was closed.

It was replaced by a ride based on *The Simpsons*, which has been refreshed over the years and remains one of the park's most popular rides.

The original thought as Disney and Universal came to Florida was that the moviemakers would follow. The dream was that Florida would become Hollywood East. Both parks built facilities for making movies and television shows, and Nickelodeon made its headquarters at Universal. Visitors could take a studio tour featuring live shows based on Nickelodeon programs. It closed in 2005 and was replaced by the Blue Man Group Theatre in 2007.

Blue Man Group was popular and regularly filled its thousand-seat theater. It fell victim to the coronavirus and closed in 2021. The television program *Swamp Thing* built sets at Universal, and the sets became an attraction when the park opened. It was part of the Production Studio Tour and lasted until 1994. In 2000, the area became the site of Men in Black: Alien Attack.

Woody Woodpecker's KidZone was a live stage show that opened with the park. It featured Universal's animal actors performing stunts. It lasted until 2001, when it was replaced with Animal Planet Live, which was inspired by the channel Animal Planet. It closed five years later to make way for Animal Actors Stage and, later, Animal Actors on Location.

Another live show was A Day in the Park with Barney, based on *Barney & Friends*. It opened in 1995. It closed in 2021 and was replaced with DreamWorks Destination, a show in which visitors were greeted by characters from DreamWorks films.

Lucy: A Tribute was a walk-through attraction highlighting the career of Lucille Ball, with visitors ending in a shop with Lucy souvenirs. It opened in 1992 and closed in 2015 and was replaced by a Hello Kitty store.

As with its California attraction, Universal hoped its Orlando park would also be a moviemaking center. It didn't work, although Nickelodeon made its headquarters there.

One of the more popular live shows was an original Dynamite Nights Stunt Spectacular, which was performed every night in the huge lagoon in the middle of the park. It took its cue from the popular television show *Miami Vice* and featured speeding boats, Jet Skis and lots of explosions. It closed after a ten-year run and was replaced by A Cinesphere Spectacular, which had fireworks, lasers and water effects and showed famous scenes from Universal movies. It ran five years before being replaced by Universal's Cinematic Spectacular: 100 Years of Movie Memories, which celebrated Universal's 100th anniversary. After five years, it gave way to Universal Orlando's Cinematic Celebration, which opened in 2018.

Just as Disney added multiple parks over the years, Universal opened a second attraction called Islands of Adventure. When it opened in 1999, it featured more thrill rides than Universal Studios. One was Dueling Dragons, which featured two inverted roller coasters. When The Wizarding World of Harry Potter opened in 2010, the ride became Dragon Challenge. After an accident in 2011, the dueling element was removed. The ride came to a stop in 2017 and was quickly torn down, to be replaced by Hagrid's Magical Creatures Motorbike Adventure.

Pandemonium Cartoon Circus opened with the park, featuring cartoon and comic strip characters. It failed to draw crowds and closed after a few months. The people coming to Islands of Adventure wanted something more exciting than cartoon characters. For Rocky and Bullwinkle, it was their second cancellation—they had already been thrown out at Universal Studios.

Mat Hoffman's Crazy Freakin' Stunt Show opened in 2002 and closed two years later. Some people objected to the word *Freakin'*, and there were other problems that led to the closing. In 2010, Hoffman returned with Mat Hoffman's Aggro Circus. It generally operated during peak seasons, such as spring break, and featured BMX bike riders and skateboarding stunts.

Few attractions have had a tougher time than the Triceratops Encounter. There were three buildings housing animatronic Triceratops named Topper, Cera and Chris. Visitors could pet the dinosaurs—if the dinosaurs were working. It closed once, reopened under the name Triceratops Discovery Trail, closed again, reopened and finally closed for good. The site became the VelociCoaster, which opened in 2021.

When Kongfrontation opened in 1990 at Universal Studios, it was one of the most popular rides. In 2002, it was replaced by Revenge of the Mummy, as Kong moved to the Islands of Adventure to become Skull Island: Reign of Kong.

The Eighth Voyage of Sinbad was one of the original attractions at Islands of Adventure in 1999. Visitors entered a grotto where Sinbad and his sidekick, Kabob, performed stunts to rescue Princess Amira from the evil Miseria. It closed in 2018.

14

THE VANISHING ATTRACTIONS

FLORIDA AFLAME

Outdoor historical dramas have had an amazing run of success in towns throughout the country. In North Carolina, there was *Unto These Hills* in the far western part of the state, while *The Lost Colony* drew big audiences on the state's east coast. In Florida, Lake Wales had the *Black Hills Passion Play*, an import from South Dakota that told about the last days of Jesus Christ, and *The Cross and the Sword* in St. Augustine was a major attraction.

Promoters convinced Safety Harbor officials to build an outdoor amphitheater and finance *Florida Aflame*, based on Florida's history. It had a huge cast of eighty-eight, and the crowds were scarce. County officials seized its assets, and the amphitheater soon rotted.

In Safety Harbor, a small town near Tampa, officials were looking for a way to draw more tourists. They were talked into building a 1,700-seat amphitheater as the site for events. In 1953, the producers of *Florida Aflame* approached officials, and two years later their play opened.

The cast was huge, with eighty-eight performers playing Indians, Americans and Spaniards, which meant a huge payroll. The crowds were small, and the bills began piling up. When paychecks were late, some cast members left. Within six months, the play was $150,000 in debt and electricity to the amphitheater lost power.

Pinellas County officials seized the *Florida Aflame* assets, including costumes, lighting equipment and furniture. The amphitheater was left to rot and in 1962 was bulldozed.

AFRICA U.S.A.

John Pedersen came to Boca Raton with ambitious plans. He developed the town of Wilton Manors then turned his attention to opening an attraction. He purchased three hundred acres at twenty-five dollars an acre and sent his son to Kenya to round up wild animals to populate Africa U.S.A. Pedersen and his son dug canals and lakes and added tens of thousands

After making his fortune in home building, John Pedersen opened Africa U.S.A. He gathered wild animals from Africa and turned his three hundred acres into a jungle. Rapid development and red ticks threatened his attraction, and it closed in 1961.

of plants to turn the property into a jungle. It opened in 1953 with emus, ostriches, elephants and giraffes. When *Life* magazine wrote a story about the growing number of theme parks, it featured Africa U.S.A on the cover instead of Disneyland. (Disney World made the *Life* cover when it opened in 1971.)

It wasn't competition from other attractions that put Africa U.S.A. out of business. It was a pair of highways. Interstate 95 and Florida's Turnpike reduced US 1 traffic. The once wide-open spaces were being devoured by housing projects that came closer and closer to the park, and the new neighbors began to complain about the noise and the occasional escape of a wild animal.

In 1961, disease-carrying red ticks were found on the animals and the park shut down.

JUNGLELAND ZOO

Competition among the state's alligator farms has always been fierce, dating back more than a century. Only a handful have survived. Jungleland Zoo built a 126-foot-long alligator out front, the largest until a 200-foot-long gator was built at Jungle Adventures in Christmas,

With a 126-foot-long alligator at the entrance, Jungleland Zoo entered the competition for Florida tourists. The owners ran into problems with government inspectors over animal treatment, and it closed in 2002.

Florida. Jungleland was replaced by Alligatorland Safari Zoo in the 1970s with more than a thousand animals and birds. The new park ran into problems with the federal government over the mistreatment of animals. The Brevard Zoological Park and Everglades Wonder Gardens were labeled the worst zoos in the country.

A surprise inspection at Alligatorland led to several charges. The owner of the park claimed it was a vendetta by the Department of Agriculture and refused to pay a $1,500 fine. After a series of court battles, Alligatorland was shut down, and Jungleland Zoo opened in 1995. Two years later, heavy rainfall flooded much of the park.

In 2002, the owners removed the animals and claimed they were victims of a severe drop-off in attendance following 9/11. There were also reports of a government investigation into the treatment of the animals.

ANCIENT AMERICA

E.G. Barnhill opened a photography business in St. Petersburg before World War I, but his true interest was American Indian culture. In 1953,

he purchased twenty-five acres near Boca Raton that included an ancient Calusa Indian mound and burial ground. His museum featured murals depicting Indian life. He tunneled into the mound and installed glass walls so visitors could see the inside of an Indian mound.

The tourists did not come, and Barnhill grew bitter. He complained that "all those tourists are

E.G. Barnhill opened Ancient America in an Indian mound near Boca Raton with murals depicting Indian life. It failed to draw, and he moved to Palm Bay, then to Kissimmee, where it closed for good after Barnhill's death.

interested in are dog tracks and nightclubs." After just a few years, he gave up in Boca Raton but tried again a few years later near Palm Bay with Indian Springs Museum.

It also failed, and he moved again, this time to Kissimmee to take advantage of the growing tourism there. The new name was the Indian World Museum and Trading Post. The new attraction was a mix of Indian artifacts, antiques and some of Barnhill's personal memorabilia. It also failed and closed in 1987, when Barnhill died at the age of ninety-three.

AQUATARIUM

The Aquatarium opened on seventeen acres in St. Petersburg Beach in 1964—just as Walt Disney was planning to open Walt Disney World. L.G. Ball, the owner of the successful Miami Seaquarium, was the developer of the St. Petersburg Beach version. There was a 160-foot geodesic dome surrounding a marine tank 100 feet in diameter.

Ball sold the attraction, and the new owners added a zoological park including lions and tigers. Following the success of the movie *Jaws*,

Aquatarium, St. Petersburg Beach, Florida - "On the Gulf of Mexico"

L.G. Ball found success with the Miami Seaquarium and opened a second attraction in St. Petersburg Beach. Ball sold the attraction, and the new owners changed the name to Shark World. It didn't help, and the park closed in 1977.

the name was changed to Shark World. It did not help, and in 1977, the park closed. The dolphins and sea lions were sent to the Miami Seaquarium.

Today, the site is the Silver Sands Beach and Racquet Club.

SIX FLAGS ATLANTIS

The developers had a grand vision: sixty-five acres in Hollywood with fantastic rides. The plans called for Atlantis the Water Kingdom to open in early 1980, but the developers ran out of money before opening day. The site sat partially completed before the giant amusement park operator Six Flags took it over in 1983. In 1989, the park was sold, and the Six Flags name was dropped. The park may have been too close to the beach—a free attraction—and bad weather often closed the park.

The new owners struggled, and after Hurricane Andrew damaged the attraction in 1992, the park closed and the rides were sold off.

The area became a shopping center, although the park's submarine was moved a few blocks away.

ATOMIC TUNNEL

This had to be one of Florida's most unusual attractions. It opened in the 1950s in Port Orange, a few miles from Daytona Beach. It was a long, tube-shaped building with 824 small windows featuring views of orchids. There were also tropical birds and a walking fish—a catfish that "walked" from one tank to another. The owner, W.R. Johnson, wanted to sell orchids and thought the tunnel would be a great gimmick. Visitors would walk through the tunnel and see the orchids in the overhead windows. They would make their selections and pay when they came through the tunnel.

People come to Florida for the sun and warm weather, and an underground attraction was not well received. The Cold War was raging, and the operators saw a way to save the attraction by adding an atomic theme.

Developers purchased sixty-five acres in Hollywood to build Atlantis the Water Kingdom. Work began, but shortly before the park was to open, the owners ran out of money. Six Flags saw an opportunity and took over but sold out in 1989. After being damaged by a hurricane, it closed in 1992.

TAKE ONE

BEAUTIFUL ATOMIC TUNNEL

DAYTONA BEACH, FLORIDA

Home of "HAPPY" the WALKING FISH

7 MILES SOUTH OF DAYTONA BEACH on U.S. Rt. 1

See "HAPPY"

TRAVEL ON LAND EVERY TOUR

You've Seen "Walking Fish" in Movies and on T.V. Now See them ALIVE

Left: At first, it was called Tropical Fantasy when it opened in the 1950s. Visitors walked through a tunnel with hundreds of small windows showing orchids that were for sale. The name was changed to Atomic Tunnel, but it did not help, and the tunnel was demolished.

Opposite: In 1953, South Dakota's Black Hills Passion Play found a winter home in Lake Wales. It was on US 27, the main tourist route, and did well until the interstate highways reduced traffic. The play closed in 1998.

The name was changed to Atomic Tunnel, and the promoters came up with a new backstory. The tunnel had been built as a bomb shelter—even with the numerous windows. The Atomic Tunnel did not draw any more visitors than the Tropical Fantasy. Another name change, to Tunnel of Fantasy, failed, and in the late 1950s, the tunnel was demolished.

THE BLACK HILLS PASSION PLAY

The tradition of plays tracing the final days of Jesus Christ began in Europe hundreds of years ago. In 1932, the passion play came to the United States and in 1939 found a permanent home in the Black Hills of South Dakota. The outdoor show was hampered by cold winter weather, and in 1953, it found a winter home in Lake Wales.

A 3,500-seat amphitheater—about half the size of the one in South Dakota—was built in an orange grove, and a cast of 25 professional actors and 250 volunteers signed on. There were camels, sheep, donkeys and horses as part of the play.

Passion plays were expensive to produce—the cast included camels, sheep, donkeys and horses—and while Lake Wales had been on the main tourist route—US 27—when it first opened, the interstate highways and Disney reduced traffic to a trickle. In 1998, the play closed. A decade later, the play in the Black Hills closed. There was an attempt to reopen it in 2002 until a series of hurricanes put it out of business for good.

Vedder Museum

The Vedder Museum in St. Augustine can claim to be Florida's oldest tourist attraction. John Vedder said he was a dentist, but much of his life is a mystery. He ended up in St. Augustine, where his original plan was to be a dentist. Instead, he opened the Vedder Museum with live alligators and snakes and what he called the "Monster Man-Eater Shark" and the "Monster Sun Fish."

His timing was good. Henry Flagler's new Ponce de Leon Hotel was drawing wealthy visitors to the city who were fascinated by attractions. They spread the word about Vedder's attraction, and the crowds came.

He died in 1899, and his museum was purchased by the St. Augustine Historical Society, which maintained it until the building burned down in 1914. Many of the creatures went to the Bronx Zoo. The society purchased the Gonzalez-Alvarez House, still referred to as "The Oldest House."

Voice in the Wind

The era of live-action plays brought *Voice in the Wind* to the Suncoast Theater in Ruskin near Tampa. Opening in 1956, it ran for two months a year telling the history of Florida. The producers convinced Hillsborough County to build an 1,800-seat amphitheater, and the state chipped in money to finance the elaborate production—perhaps too elaborate. The investment totaled over $100,000. There were twenty-nine scenes, a cast

The Vedder Museum dates to the 1800s, claiming to be the first tourist attraction in Florida. It was a collection of a St. Augustine dentist including the Monster Sun Fish.

Voice in the Wind had a brief life in Ruskin in the mid-1950s. Hillsborough County built an 1,800-seat amphitheater, and a huge cast was assembled. The producers ran out of money, and the play closed.

of fifty-five actors and 120 costumes. Its run was brief. Ruskin was isolated in the 1950s, and the expenses mounted and the play closed.

EVERGLADES GATORLAND

Everglades Gatorland was one of the dozens of attractions along US 27 when the highway through the middle of Florida was the prime route for tourists. It began as a gas station in South Bay near the southern shore of Lake Okeechobee. The thousands of drivers heading for Miami passed it each day. The tourists often stopped because they could see alligators in the lake behind the station. In 1959, J.C. Bowen captured some of the gators and soon added ocelots and even a vulture. Even as US 27 declined as a route through the state, Everglades Gatorland stayed in business while other small attractions failed. In 1967, the state passed regulations governing the treatment of captive animals, including a minimum pen size. That forced the attraction to make changes; just as the cost of feeding the gators increased, traffic declined, and by 1991, the owners could not find any buyers. It became overgrown, and the cages were emptied and abandoned. Finally, in 2020, what remained was torn down.

WEBB'S CITY

It was Walmart before there was Walmart, and it became a tourist attraction, sprawling four city blocks in downtown St. Petersburg. Doc Webb started with Doc's Original Drugstore in 1925 in the middle of the Florida land boom.

Not only did he survive the land bust in the late 1920s, he also expanded during the Great Depression. What began as a 17-by-28-foot space soon covered several blocks. By 1951, his store covered 85,000 square feet (the average Walmart is 105,000 square feet) and police had to direct traffic in the two-thousand-car lot. At its height, it drew sixty thousand customers a day.

Doc Webb opened his drugstore during the 1920s and for the next half century expanded. He sold nearly everything and tried every gimmick to make a sale.

LOST ATTRACTIONS OF FLORIDA

Webb was a brilliant self-promoter whose motto was "Stack it high and sell it cheap." There were haircuts for a quarter and an entire breakfast for two cents. He once sold dollar bills for ninety-five cents, and there was entertainment, including ducks playing baseball and a dancing chicken.

On August 18, 1979, the doors were closed for the last time. The store, including its giant mermaid sign, remained until it and the building were torn down five years later.

BONGOLAND

It began as a one-thousand-acre plantation near present-day Daytona Beach in 1804, and in 1832, the Dunlawton Sugar Mill began operations. It passed through several hands, and with nearly every change in ownership, it was divided into smaller portions. In the 1940s, Dr. Perry Sperber purchased some of the land. He was a dermatologist with a passion for dinosaurs, even writing a book titled *Sex and the Dinosaur*.

He turned his property into a theme park with huge concrete dinosaurs and other prehistoric animals. There was a Seminole village and live animals, including a baboon named Bongo. Sperber used a miniature train to transport his visitors through the attraction.

The attraction failed to draw visitors and closed in 1952. Several of the concrete dinosaurs remain, standing in what is now Dunlawton Sugar Mill Gardens.

CAPE CORAL GARDENS

In the late 1950s, Leonard and Jack Rosen purchased a huge tract of land near Fort Myers to create a massive housing development. Much of it was swampland, and the two had to dig miles of canals before they began selling the first of thousands of lots. Their challenge was to draw potential buyers to their out-of-the-way development and get a chance to sell them a lot and a home. The result was Cape Coral Gardens, an eighty-acre attraction. When it opened in 1964, it had a porpoise show, gardens including forty thousand rose bushes, animal exhibits and a Waltzing Waters fountain show. Cape Coral was a success and eventually was home to eight hundred thousand people.

Bongoland began as a sprawling plantation in 1804. In the 1940s, it became a theme park with large concrete dinosaurs. The star was a baboon named Bongo. It closed in 1952.

Cape Coral Gardens included a replica of the Iwo Jima Memorial to draw prospective homebuyers.

The Waltzing Waters was originally located at Cape Coral Gardens then moved to North Cape Coral in 1971.

The brothers no longer needed Cape Coral Gardens to draw potential buyers, and the land it consumed had become valuable. The attraction was closed and the land turned into an upscale neighborhood. The Waltzing Waters became the Waltzing Waters Aquarama.

The Waltzing Waters moved to a site in North Cape Coral and opened in 1971. It was a series of fountains brightly illuminated that shot into the air accompanied by music. There were other water-based attractions, including dolphins and sea lions.

The timing was terrible, opening the same year as Disney World and featuring passive attractions for tourists who wanted exciting rides. After nearly two decades, the attraction closed, although the owners continue to make fountains for others.

CROSS AND SWORD

In 1937, the Pulitzer Prize–winning playwright Paul Green wrote a play about Walter Raleigh's Roanoke colony titled *Lost Colony*. It told a dramatic story and included music and dance and a huge cast. Green was asked to write a play about the European conquest of Florida, and a two-thousand-

Cross and Sword was once Florida's official state play, with a large cast and a popular following. The St. Augustine play lost its state funding and closed in 1996.

seat amphitheater was built in St. Augustine for *Cross and Sword*. It told the story of the early days of the Spanish in Florida and the battles with the French. The play was a success and became Florida's official state play. The costs of producing the play were high, reflecting the large cast, the elaborate costumes—there were 250 costumes—and the fact that performances were limited to the summer months and subject to being canceled by inclement weather. In the mid-1990s, the state cut funding for the play, and the aging amphitheater needed renovation. The play closed in 1996. In 2002, the amphitheater was taken over by St. Johns County and turned into an entertainment venue.

Cypress Knee Museum

Tom Gaskins was one of the dozens of men and women who started tourist attractions based on things they liked—and hoped others would share their interest. For five decades, Gaskins operated his Cypress Knee Museum about fifty miles east of Fort Myers. In 1939, he displayed his cypress knees at the Florida Pavilion and held the only patent on manufacturing cypress knees.

He bragged that it had the world's largest collection of knobby cypress upgrowths—and, of course, it was the only collection in the world. It began with fifty acres in Palmdale he leased for fifteen dollars a year from the Lykes Brothers, a giant citrus and ranching company. His museum opened in 1951 along US 27, the prime tourist route in the state. He erected signs made of dead cypress trees and installed them along the highway and built a walkway through the swamps. The Highway Beautification Act of 1965 forced him to remove his cypress billboards, and other laws limited the cutting of cypress trees. In 1993, Tom Gaskins retired and his son Tom Gaskins Jr. took over. When the elder Tom died in 1998, his deal with the Lykes Brothers died with him, and the property was sold to the state under a preservation program. The property was repeatedly vandalized, and many of the knees were stolen. The remains of the building still stand.

Tom Gaskins really liked cypress tree knees and made them his life work. He operated his Cypress Knee Museum for nearly fifty years. After his death, his property passed to the state.

DIXIE STAMPEDE

Dixie Stampede was an extension of singer Dolly Parton's entertainment empire. The park opened in 2003 and drew decent crowds to the one-thousand-seat arena a few miles from Disney World. The show featured a mix of animals and action, including a Civil War battle. It was hurt because it did not serve alcohol, unlike its competitors, Medieval Times and Arabian Nights.

It closed without notice in January 2008 and was sold to an outlet mall developer. For weeks, employees had heard rumors as the company denied any plans to close just hours before the closure was announced. The operators announced that they were seeking another location in Orlando. Parton herself said, "We will be back better than ever!" There were no further announcements about a new location.

With a Civil War theme, it was caught in a changing world. Parton may have realized the changing times. She dropped the word *Dixie* from the name in her other locations and revamped the show in Myrtle Beach, South Carolina, to Pirates Voyage Dinner Theater.

MYSTERY FUN HOUSE

It was the creation of time-share mogul David Siegel and survived for twenty-five years during changing tourism patterns. The Mystery Fun House opened in 1976 at the entrance to Siegel's time-share check-in center. It sat on fifteen acres and included a mirror maze, crawl-through tunnels and a crooked room. Over time, an arcade, miniature golf course and laser-tag attractions were added. As Siegel's empire grew, his need for an attraction to lure guests declined, and it was overshadowed by a dozen other attractions. It finally closed in 2001.

SANLANDO SPRINGS

Most of the early springs attractions ended up as public spaces, but Sanlando Springs was privately owned from the 1930s to the 1970s and open to the public for a small fee. In 1970, the land was sold to private developers who turned it into an upscale development known as The Springs. The Springs, outside of Orlando, is open only to residents of the community.

Above: In the early days of time-shares, one promoter needed help drawing potential customers. He created Mystery Fun House in Orlando. It worked, and he created a national time-share empire.

Right: Many springs are owned by the State of Florida today, but one became a private housing development. Sanlando Springs near Orlando was privately owned until 1970, when it was sold to developers.

Rainbow Springs

It was known as Blue Springs until the 1930s, when it opened as a tourist attraction called Rainbow Springs. The springs had to compete with the far better-known Silver Springs, which was nearby. Instead of the famous glass-bottom boats at Silver Springs, Rainbow Springs featured submarine tours and launched the first mermaid shows. The springs closed as a tourist attraction in the 1970s and remained in private hands until 1990, when the state acquired the springs to save the area from development. Today, it is Rainbow Springs State Park.

Xanadu House

It was to be the home of the future, but the future came faster than its builders could imagine. Beginning in 1979, three futuristic homes were built in resort areas: Wisconsin Dells, Wisconsin; Gatlinburg, Tennessee; and Kissimmee, Florida.

They were constructed using polyurethane insulation foam instead of concrete. Inside, there were home-automation systems. The home electronics were controlled by Commodore computers, which were at first cutting edge and later little more than toys. In its early years, it drew one thousand visitors a day, enough to be profitable. The homes in Wisconsin Dells and Gatlinburg failed to attract enough visitors and were closed.

The Kissimmee home cost $300,000 to build. When it opened in 1983, it had over six thousand square feet of living space. Huge balloons were used to build the house. The balloons were inflated, and polyurethane foam was sprayed around them. Then the air was let out of the balloons.

The house was a steady draw until 1990, when the home of the future became dated. Technology that seemed so cutting edge in the 1970s seemed almost cartoonish by 1990. In humid Florida, mold became a problem, and the home closed in 1996. It was sold in 1997 and converted into office and storage space. Eventually, it was abandoned and became decrepit and a home for the homeless. In 2005, it was torn down.

In the 1930s, Rainbow Springs became a tourist attraction complete with submarine tours and mermaids. The state acquired the land in 1990.

Xanadu House was designed to be the home of the future. Made of polyurethane insulation foam, it once had locations in Wisconsin, Gatlinburg and Kissimmee. The house quickly became dated and closed in 1996.

Clyde Beatty's Jungle Zoo

George Hamid started his career in entertainment as a child working with Buffalo Bill's Wild West Show shortly after the turn of the century. By 1932, he had his own circus, the Hamid-Morton Circus, and needed a winter home for his acts. In 1956, he purchased Tropical Panorama, a small, struggling attraction in Miami. He added water attractions and changed the name to Aquafair.

Hamid and his son George Jr. held the concession at Atlantic City—home of the high-diving horse—and they thought they would create something similar in Florida. After two years, attendance fell, and Hamid gave up in 1959. He turned the attraction over to the legendary lion tamer Clyde Beatty, who had left home to join a circus in 1921 and soon was billed as "America's youngest and most fearless wild animal trainer." Beatty became one of the best-known circus performers in history. Armed with a chair, a whip and a pistol, he entered lion cages for decades. As his fame increased, he had a radio show (an actor provided his voice), appeared in movies and, later, television and had his own circus. In 1939, Beatty purchased the McKillop-Hutton Lion Farm in Fort Lauderdale. He turned the land into the winter home for his circus and an attraction. He called it Clyde Beatty's Jungle Zoo and found some success. In the post–World War II world, Fort Lauderdale was growing, and neighbors complained of noise and traffic. Beatty hit the road with his show. He thought he found a home in DeLeon Springs, but it fell through. In 1960, he leased Aquafair, a small tourist attraction in North Miami. He spent months renovating and opened his park in 1960. Success eluded him, and his park lasted just a year. Beatty died of cancer in 1965.

Circus Hall of Fame

When John Ringling came to Sarasota after World War I, it was little more than a sleepy fishing village. Ringling saw potential and began the process that would turn it into a world-famous resort. He created a winter headquarters for his circus and built a magnificent mansion. Year after year, the circus came back, and by the 1950s, a move was started to create a circus museum and hall of fame. The museum began with a single item, a giant circus wagon built in 1896 that required forty horses to pull it. Along with other donations, the Circus Hall of Fame opened in 1956. There were

Clyde Beatty became the nation's most famous lion tamer, but he had
little luck with his Florida attractions. He started by acquiring an existing
attraction, but attendance fell, and after more attempts, he gave up in 1961.

John Ringling chose Sarasota for the winter home for his circus, and the town became synonymous with the circus. In 1956, the Circus Hall of Fame opened and drew crowds until the 1970s, when attendance declined.

daily performances by various circus acts. Artifacts included Annie Oakley's guns and Tom Thumb's coach. The museum did well until the 1970s, when attendance declined and the museum owners decided to sell their building. The final performance came in 1980.

MIAMI SERPENTARIUM

Drivers on Miami's South Dixie Highway first noticed the thirty-five-foot-high cobra made of concrete and stucco. Below was the Miami Serpentarium, which opened in 1947 and drew a steady stream of about fifty thousand visitors a year. It was founded by Bill Haast, who became interested in snakes as a child. In New Jersey, his mother had a concession stand at a lakeside resort, and Haast convinced her to let him add a snake exhibit. He was always thinking bigger, and he moved to Florida to open a snake farm. His dream gave way to reality; his wife was pregnant and he needed a steady job. He became a mechanic and moved to Miami to work for Pan American World Airways. Despite the steady work, he kept his dream alive. In 1946, he purchased a plot of land on US 1 south of Miami.

The Serpentarium eventually housed five hundred snakes. Visitors watched as Haast extracted venom from the snakes. As a sideline, he supplied venom to the University of Miami for experiments. In 1977, a six-year-old boy fell into the crocodile pit and was killed. Although Haast killed the crocodile, the incident left him depressed. He removed the crocodiles, but the joy of owning the park was over. He closed the Serpentarium in 1984 and later established the Miami Serpentarium Laboratories to sell venom.

The Miami Serpentarium opened in 1947 and was a hit. It had hundreds of snakes and alligators. The park closed to the public in 1984 and became a laboratory selling snake venom.

TRAGEDY IN US HISTORY MUSEUM

St. Augustine is the oldest city in the United States. It is full of history, both real and imagined. One of the strangest St. Augustine attractions was the Tragedy in US History Museum. Buddy Hough opened his attraction in a city that didn't want his museum. His museum, full of depressing oddities, was not the image the city wanted to project, and city leaders fought the museum in a struggle that went all the way to the Florida Supreme Court. It finally opened in a small house with a large sign proclaiming "See Jayne Mansfield's death car." The museum included the bedroom furniture from Lee Harvey Oswald's house, a copy of Elvis Presley's will and a mummy in a coffin. There were human skeletons and the Bonnie and Clyde death car. (Actually, it was the car from the movie, not the one Bonnie and Clyde died in.)

Hough died in 1996, and his widow kept the museum open for two more years. Hough's collection of misery was sold at auction. St. Augustine never accepted the attraction; tourist trams passed by without mentioning the attraction.

TUSSAUD'S LONDON WAX MUSEUM

Tussaud's London Wax Museum opened in St. Petersburg Beach in 1963 with more than 120 wax figures from history, horror and entertainment. The founder was Alec Rigby, who was a partner in Ripley's Believe It or Not! Its

Tussaud's London Wax Museum opened in St. Petersburg Beach in 1963 with 120 figures. It drew crowds on rainy days, but it was not enough, and it closed in 1989.

relationship to Madam Tussaud was murky. At times, it called itself Louis Tussaud's London Wax Museum or advertised as "From Josephine Tussaud of England." The museum did well on rainy days, but when the sun was shining, people headed for the beaches or other attractions. In 1978, the museum was sold, and the new owner added Freddy Krueger and Rambo figures to update the attraction. As Disney opened and Busch Gardens added rides, the wax museum attendance declined. In 1989, the museum closed. There were supposed to be plans to move to another location on the state's west coast, but it never happened. The wax figures were sold to other museums, except for the figure of baseball great Stan Musial, whose wax figure was sold to his widow.

Stars Hall of Fame

Allen Parkinson made a fortune inventing Sleep-Eze, a sleep aid, in 1948. He sold the company in 1959 and decided to get into the attractions business. He opened Movieland Wax Museum near Disneyland in 1962 and saw a million visitors a year come through the doors. He sold out to Six Flags in 1970 and made yet another fortune. Six Flags was in an acquiring mood, buying Atlantis in Florida, Autoworld in Michigan and an entertainment center in Maryland. They were all poor choices and failed. Still, Six Flags pushed ahead and thought it could clone Movieland in Orlando just a few miles from Disney World and right on the interstate highway. It was called Six Flags Stars Hall of Fame Wax Museum—an unwieldy title. It contained more than two hundred mostly static wax figures, although some had minimal movement. The attraction was a fair draw throughout the 1970s, but then attendance began to drop off. The opening of EPCOT in 1981 sent the museum's attendance through the floor, and Six Flags wanted out. It found a willing buyer in Harcourt Brace Jovanovich. Harcourt Brace was formed after World War I and became a major force in publishing.

In 1955, William Jovanovich was named president and began turning the old-line publisher into a conglomerate. In 1970, he changed the name of the company to Harcourt Brace Jovanovich and stepped up his acquisitions.

Many of the acquisitions were poor, and some had nothing to do with publishing, including his entry into tourism. Jovanovich snapped up a series of attractions, including Stars Hall of Fame. He didn't want the attraction— he wanted the building and the land, which was near the HBJ building. In

With the coming of Disney World, promoters lined up to open attractions in Orlando. One was Stars Hall of Fame, a wax museum just a few miles from Disney. It could not compete with more exciting attractions and closed in 1984.

1984, the wax museum closed and the building became the HBJ World of Learning, a display of the company's extensive educational tools. The wild spending spree of Jovanovich left the company in debt, and it was forced to sell off its attractions. The Hall of Fame property—along with nearby SeaWorld—went to Busch Entertainment. Busch had no use for the building, and eventually the hall of fame property went to developers.

SUNKEN GARDENS

St. Petersburg's Sunken Gardens is one of Florida's longest-surviving attractions. In 1903, George Turner purchased six acres with a small lake in the northeast neighborhood of the city. He drained the lake and used the bed to create his "sunken" gardens. He planted papayas and citrus trees and in the 1920s opened a nursery. He charged visitors a nickel to see his gardens in the 1930s and put up fences to keep out those who might not want to pay.

Sunken Gardens was a nursery before opening to tourists in the 1930s, and it became a top tourist attraction. The City of St. Petersburg acquired the land.

By the 1950s, the gardens were among the state's top ten attractions. Turner died in 1961, and his sons took over the property. They acquired a former Coca-Cola Bottling Company plant in 1967 and converted it into what they called the World's Largest Gift Shop and added a small wax museum. In 1999, the sons sold their property to the City of St. Petersburg for $2.3 million. The city converted the building into a children's museum and began maintaining the gardens.

ROSS ALLEN'S REPTILE INSTITUTE

When Ross Allen was a Boy Scout, he earned several wildlife merit badges and dedicated his life to wildlife. When *Tarzan* movies were filmed in Florida, Allen was a stand-in for Johnny Weissmuller and even starred in some short films. He became friends with Marjorie Kinnan Rawlings and took her snake-hunting while she was working on her book *Cross Creek*. In 1929, he founded Ross Allen's Reptile Institute at Silver Springs, where he displayed snakes, alligators and an Indian village with Seminole Indians.

After watching the show, the tourists could purchase baby alligators to take home. Over time, he became more interested in research. He began milking the snakes and selling venom to be used for research and antivenin. He raised snakes to be sold to zoos and other tourist attractions.

For half a century, Ross Allen was a fixture in Florida tourism with his snake shows. He died shortly before opening an attraction in Lake City.

For more than a century, Silver Springs has brought tourists to Florida to ride the glass-bottom boats. This photo shows the springs being used to film a movie.

Business boomed until the opening of Disney World. Silver Springs had spawned several nearby attractions, and those began to disappear. Tommy Bartlett's Deer Ranch, the Prince of Peace Memorial and the Reptile Institute either closed or were absorbed into the main Silver Springs. Ross moved to the Alligator Farm in St. Augustine and let a small park in North Fort Myers use his name. He began planning bigger things: Ross Allen's Alligator Town was to be a major attraction in Lake City at the intersection of I-75 and US 90. He purchased fifty acres and spent $800,000 creating his attraction with his traditional snake and alligator shows, but also waterslides, rides and an amphitheater for concerts. He was betting that families on their way to Disney from the Midwest would want a break and would stop 150 miles from their destination. As opening day approached, Allen became ill and died one month before opening day. When it did open, it struggled and closed after the turn of the century.

PIRATES WORLD

Pirates World had bad timing. It opened in 1967, just as construction began on Disney World two hundred miles to the north. Promoters purchased one hundred acres in Dania, and the park featured an observation tower called The Crow's Nest, which had been the Belgian Aerial Tower at the New York World's Fair.

There was a pirate ship ride in a life-sized pirate ship. It sailed along a waterway as cannons fired around it and enemy pirates attempted to board the ship. There were other rides, a petting zoo and a seal pond. It also featured carnival games such as Skee-Ball. Pirates World also featured regular concerts with dozens of best-selling groups including The Moody Blues, The Guess Who, The Doors and Led Zeppelin. The park did well

Pirates World occupied one hundred acres in Dania and combined rides and with regular concerts and lots of cannons. In 1973, the owners declared bankruptcy.

until 1971, when Disney opened and attendance plummeted. In 1973, the park's owners declared bankruptcy. Nothing came of plans to build a biblical theme park, and condos and homes were built on the site.

MIAMI RARE BIRD FARM

The most famous resident of the Miami Rare Bird Farm was Enos, a chimpanzee who made the first orbital space flight for the United States on November 29, 1961. The seven-acre attraction opened in 1938 and was owned by Alton Freeman, a retired U.S. State Department employee who wanted to get into the business of selling animals to zoos and movies. Freeman purchased the land for $40,000 and established his animal farm. He found success and decided to expand and admit tourists. There was a giant walk-in aviary, where visitors could feed the birds. Although Freeman was successful, development around the attraction drove up land prices, and the Freeman family sold the land in 1961. Freeman moved to Spruce Pine, North Carolina, where he opened an animal refuge. His attraction site was divided into residential and commercial properties.

Miami Rare Bird Farm was one of the early South Florida attractions, opening in 1938. The attraction was a success, but rising land prices made the property more valuable, and the owners sold out to developers.

FLORIDALAND

Just one year after Walt Disney secretly selected Orlando as the site of his new attraction, Floridaland opened near Sarasota. Nearly five thousand people showed up that first day in 1964 to see the park with "Everything under the sun."

Developers purchased 50 acres (Disney was in the process of buying 27,000 acres) and predicted that two hundred thousand people would come each year. The park bragged that it was ten parks in one place. There was a Western ghost town, porpoise shows, an Indian village, wagon rides and a riverboat. The park hoped to be all things to all people on a thin budget.

Floridaland seemed to have everything but ended up going broke. It closed just as Disney World was opening.

The result is that everything seemed to be cheap. The Western train was a tram dressed up to look like a train. Holiday Inn opened a one-hundred-room hotel to serve Floridaland, and more development was promised. By 1968, attendance was declining, the operating dates were reduced and the skyride closed. The park closed just as Disney World was opening.

JAMES MELTON'S AUTORAMA

James Melton made his name as an entertainer, singing on radio and television, in movies and in the New York Metropolitan Opera. By the early 1950s, he had his own NBC show, *Ford Festival*, and was a regular on Jack Benny's radio show. His true love was the automobile. Melton began the tradition of singing "Back Home Again in Indiana" at the Indianapolis 500.

James Melton was a famous singer who used his money to collect cars. He put his collection on display in Hypoluxo in the 1950s. It closed in 1961 after his death.

He began collecting cars and, in the 1950s, put his collection on display in Hypoluxo. He owned nearly one hundred antique automobiles, along with toys, music boxes and baby carriages. When he died in 1961, the museum was closed.

THE *HMS* BOUNTY

The 1962 remake of *Mutiny on the Bounty* was a colossal flop and nearly put the studio that made it into bankruptcy. It was compared unfavorably to the 1935 original with Clark Gable. The best part of the movie was the magnificent ship built for the film. The ship was used to promote the movie then sailed to St. Petersburg to dock. It remained in St. Petersburg until the mid-1980s as a tourist attraction. In 1986, the media mogul Ted Turner purchased MGM's film library, and the ship came with the deal.

Turner donated it to the Fall River Chamber Foundation. It spent summers in New England and winters in St. Petersburg. It was also used to make a few movies. The aging ship was in desperate need of repair, and

The HMS *Bounty* was built for a movie then became a Tampa attraction. It had a tragic ending, sinking in a hurricane.

there was not enough money. The ship went to a foundation, and repairs were made. In 2012, the ship left New London, Connecticut, headed for its winter berth in St. Petersburg. It ran into Hurricane Sandy and sank off the coast of North Carolina. The ship's captain and a crewmember were lost.

Gerbing Gardens

In 1937, Gustav Gerbing transformed seven acres of his family land along the Amelia River into a public garden. Once he finished with the seven acres, he began expanding with azaleas and other plants throughout the dozen acres his father had purchased in 1897. Visitors could buy the plants or enjoy the view. As word of his gardens spread, he began to ship plants throughout the country. Gerbing said he had one hundred thousand azaleas. The land was sold and developed, although signs of the original gardens remain.

Gustav Gerbing turned his passion into an attraction with more than one hundred thousand azaleas. As the land became valuable, developers moved in.

FLORIDA REPTILE LAND

There were hundreds of gas stations along Florida's highways, and the problem for the owners was getting people to stop at their stations. Many added amenities such as a restaurant and souvenirs and found that adding animals was the surest way to draw a crowd. Florida Reptile Land was near Jacksonville on US 301, then a major thoroughfare for drivers heading south. (There was also a Florida Reptile Land in Perry.) Florida Reptile Land had a huge sign and some animals, and that was enough. Admission to these stops was almost always free; but with kids in tow, it was difficult to get out without spending money. A prime attraction was a talented chicken. If a coin was deposited into the chicken's cage, the chicken rang a bell and corn was dispensed. The interstate highways reduced tourist traffic to a trickle, and Florida Reptile Land closed in 1984.

WONDER HOUSE

Conrad Schuck came from Pennsylvania in 1926 and settled in Bartow on fourteen acres. His doctors told him he had a short time to live and suggested that moving to Florida might help. When he moved to Bartow in the 1920s, he wanted to build a home but found that lumber was in short supply. He decided to use steel rails the railroad did not need as well as stone, which was plentiful in the bedrock beneath his property.

The hard work rejuvenated Schuck—he lived for another forty years—and he designed his home to be well ventilated to help during the Florida summers. The house had four stories, a basement and a subbasement. He ended up with an eighteen-room house that was never entirely done.

In 1934, he opened it to tourists, charging ten cents for admission. It was just minutes from US 27, the main Florida tourist route in the 1930s. It remained a tourist attraction until 1963.

In 1964, the house was sold to the DuCharme family, which completed work on the house and added central air and heat. The last member of the family died in 1999, and the house passed to Chuck and Helen Heiden, who began restoring it. Their ambitious plans ended when the couple divorced in 2012, and the home was abandoned. During the next three years, it was purchased and abandoned by two buyers. Finally, Drew Davis and Krislin Kreis purchased the house in 2015 at auction for just $162,750. They offer special tours by advance arrangement.

There were two Florida Reptile Land attractions, one near Jacksonville and another in Perry. They offered the same things: alligators and snakes.

Conrad Schuck built one of the state's most unusual homes and turned it into a tourist attraction in Bartow. It was on a popular tourist route and drew tourists with its ten-cent admission.

DUPREE GARDENS

Dupree Gardens opened in 1940 near Tampa and became a hit, drawing thirty thousand visitors a year to what became known as the "Blossom Center of Florida." It began as twenty-five acres of beautiful flowers with waterfalls, streams and glass-bottom boats. The gardens were developed by J.W. Dupree, a Tampa attorney who owned a nine-hundred-acre estate. By 1948, the American Automobile Association called it one of Florida's major attractions. In the 1950s, Dupree sold the land, and it became homesites, citrus groves and even a nudist colony.

Dupree Gardens opened on the eve of World War II and became popular. But the land near Tampa was valuable, and the family sold it in the 1950s.

TOMMY BARTLETT'S INTERNATIONAL DEER RANCH

Tommy Bartlett began as a radio announcer and host of Chicago radio programs. In 1949, he went to his first water-ski show, which inspired him to start a touring water-ski show. He found a permanent home for his show in Wisconsin Dells and drew thousands of fans each year. In 1954, he opened Tommy Bartlett's International Deer Ranch on the Silver Springs property. Just as Disney World would lead other attractions to be built nearby, Silver Springs was a draw for other attractions. While the deer were the main draw, there were also chickens capable of telling fortunes

Tommy Bartlett started his water-ski show in Wisconsin then opened his International Deer Ranch in Silver Springs. The deer ranch closed in 1975.

and dancing and drum-playing ducks. The deer ranch shared a parking lot with Silver Springs, and visitors to the springs could ride a Christmas-themed trailer to the deer ranch.

Bartlett and the owners of Silver Springs had a falling out, and Bartlett decided to concentrate on his Wisconsin Dells attraction. Silver Springs absorbed the deer ranch in 1975.

Prince of Peace Memorial

Like Tommy Bartlett's International Deer Ranch, the Prince of Peace Memorial was part of the sprawling Silver Springs. Artist Paul Cunningham came in the mid-1950s and created a dozen hand-carved scenes from the life of Christ. He built a bell tower and a chapel and shared a parking lot with Silver Springs. Initially, adults paid fifty cents and children a quarter to walk through the scenes. It lasted into the 1970s.

Lewis Plantation

The Lewis Plantation in Brooksville captured old Florida, for better or worse. Pearce Lewis operated a turpentine still on his twenty-five acres when Florida was one of the largest turpentine producers in the country. In the 1930s, Lewis ran into financial problems as demand for turpentine declined during the Great Depression.

He turned his plantation into a tourist attraction, thinking visitors would like to see what post–Civil War Florida was like. He hired local African Americans to play former slaves and even featured "Pickaninnies at Play."

For a time, the plantation was a success, and tourists paid fifteen cents to ride on a mule-drawn wagon. As the modern civil rights movement began in the 1950s, the Lewis plantation seemed terribly wrong. By the end of the decade, the attraction was closed.

Prince of Peace Memorial featured hand-carved scenes from the life of Christ. It was located next to Silver Springs. It closed in the 1970s.

Pearce Lewis thought tourists would like to see what old Florida was like. For a time, it was a success but gave way to changing times.

McKee Botanical Garden

In 1929, Arthur McKee purchased eighty acres on the Indian River in the small community of Vero Beach. He hired a landscape architect to design gardens with streams, ponds and trails. He gathered seeds for tropical plants from around the world, and in 1932 he opened his gardens, known as McKee Jungle Gardens. He added monkeys, elephants and other wild creatures. It was the perfect place for tourists to stop for a break in the drive to Miami. By the 1940s, the gardens drew one hundred thousand visitors a year.

As the interstate highway came and air travel became more popular, attendance declined. The gardens closed in 1976 and fell into disrepair. By the 1990s, the land was to be cleared for a shopping center. The residents of Vero Beach raised $1.7 million to buy the land and save the gardens. The new gardens were dedicated in 2001. Today, the gardens feature one of the largest collections of water lilies, and there are ten thousand species of plants and trees.

Pioneer City

When Mike Weiss came up with the idea for Pioneer City in the mid-1960s, the Western was still riding high on television and in the movies. His idea was to build a model of Dodge City in Davie, with shootouts at high noon, barroom brawls and even hangings for the bad guys. Weiss owned a massive five thousand acres in what was then rural Broward County. He chose two hundred acres for his park and built it to exact specifications over two years. A nineteenth-century steam locomotive was purchased, and two paddle-wheel boats were built. Weiss seemed to have planned everything except the weather.

When it opened in 1966, there were heavy rains—twenty-one inches in the first month. There were also traffic problems, and within two years, the park closed. Much of it was demolished to make way for a Kapok Tree restaurant, an attraction itself. The restaurant operated from 1974 to 1990. Today, it is the site of the county-run Long Key Natural Area and Nature Center.

Right: Arthur McKee built his beautiful gardens in Vero Beach in 1929. They were popular until the 1970s, when competition from Disney and changing highway patterns led to its closure.

Below: Pioneer City was one of the Western-themed attractions that followed the rise of Western television programs. It opened in 1966 and experienced constant weather problems and closed within two years.

OCALA CAVERNS

There are plenty of stories about the Ocala Caverns, beginning with claims that runaway slaves sought refuge in the caves during the Civil War. Ocala Caverns was a quarry during the first decades of the twentieth century. In 1953, the property was purchased by Edmond Heintz, who turned it into Magic Valley and Coral Caves. In 1958, the ownership and the name changed. It became Uranium Valley and Caves. The nuclear arms race was on, and *uranium* was a magical name. Not only could it destroy nations, but it was also supposed to be good for the skin. Clifford Jack took over and changed the name back to Ocala Caverns and made significant improvements, including installing boats and lights. The property changed hands again in 1965, when a professional wrestler known as Man Mountain Dean Jr., who weighed 650 pounds, took over. He added an Inca Indian Museum, Santa Claus Land and even a Wrestling Hall of Fame. A giant statue of Man Mountain stood in front of the entrance. When he died in 1972, the caverns closed and fell into disrepair. The Florida Speleological Society has worked to clean up the site recently.

ORIENTAL GARDENS

In 1925, real estate developer George W. Clark began planting his botanical collection on a bluff overlooking the St. Johns River. It was a private garden until Clark opened it to the public in 1937. The gardens became a popular attraction featuring nearly one hundred varieties of plants, trees and shrubs. There were also concerts to draw visitors. Jacksonville was booming, and there was a demand for the property. Clark's widow sold it to developers in 1945, and in 1954, the beautiful gardens were carved into thirty-three homesites.

MUSA ISLE SEMINOLE INDIAN VILLAGE

Chief Willie Willie opened the Seminole Indian Village in 1917 on the Miami River at Northwest Twenty-Fifth Avenue, near what is today Little Havana. At the time, it was mostly a farming area. It featured a Seminole

Ocala Caverns was a quarry in the early twentieth century. In 1953, the property was opened to the public. At one time, a 650-pound wrestler owned it.

Oriental Gardens started as a private garden in 1925, then began admitting tourists in 1937. A dozen years later, the land was sold for homesites.

Musa Isle Seminole Indian Village was one of the first attractions, opening in 1917 in Miami. It featured Seminole Indians showing how they lived.

village, along with alligator wrestling. It was reached by crude roads or a sightseeing boat sailing up the Miami River. In the days before casinos, the Seminoles relied on tourism, making crafts and selling trinkets. Willie opened other Seminole attractions, but Miami was growing, and the land around Musa Isle was becoming more valuable. Musa Isle was sold several times before closing in 1964.

COPPINGER'S PIRATE'S COVE

This was one of South Florida's first attractions. Henry Coppinger was born in Ireland and opened his Miami attraction in 1917 on the Miami River. Efforts to drain the Everglades had hurt the ability of the Seminole Indians to hunt and fish, and they established a camp inside the attraction and sold handmade souvenirs, with small, ten-cent Indian dolls being the favorite.

The Seminoles had been hunters who sold animal pelts before efforts to drain the Everglades destroyed their hunting grounds. It opened the same year as the nearby Musa Isle Seminole Indian Village. Like Musa, it began as a tropical garden with a citrus grove. Boats traveling along the Miami River could stop and allow passengers a glass of orange juice. Coppinger introduced alligator wrestling, and Musa soon followed. Coppinger's son became known as the "Alligator Boy" for his wrestling expertise.

LAKE PLACID TOWER

In 1938, Earnest Oakley moved to Orlando with plans to build an observation tower as a tourist attraction. The war came, and his plans were shelved. In 1947, he moved to Sebring and revived his plan for a tower.

In 1960, his dream came through. The tower was 240 feet high and built with one hundred thousand concrete blocks. The local chamber of commerce opened an office at the base, and there was a gift shop, a motel, a restaurant and a gas station. Attendance lagged—from 240 feet, there wasn't a lot to see—and the name was changed to The Happiness Tower amid promises that bliss could be found at the top.

The owners fell behind on their taxes, and the tower closed in 1982. The owners tried to boost attendance in 1986 by adding a petting zoo. Attendance remained low, and it closed again. A new owner tried again from 1992 to 2003, when it closed for good. It was sold for use as a cellphone tower.

PLANET OCEAN

Planet Ocean opened in the 1970s across the street from the Miami Seaquarium on Virginia Key. It was an eighty-thousand-square-foot interactive oceanographic museum. There were dozens of displays of submersibles, a touchable piece of an iceberg and educational experiences. Perhaps it was too educational, and fun seekers preferred the Seaquarium across the street. Planet Ocean closed in 1991. The building now houses the Rosenstiel School of Marine and Atmospheric Sciences, which is part of the University of Miami.

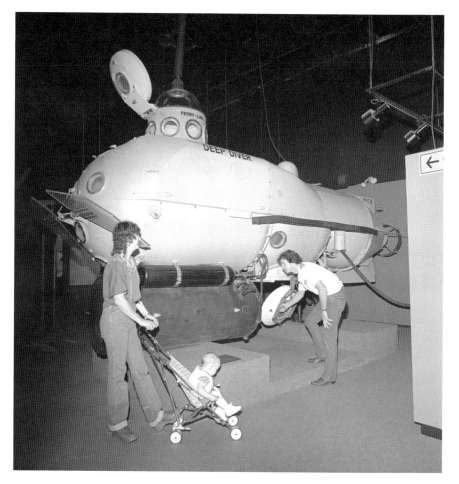

Planet Ocean opened in the 1970s but could not compete with the more exciting Miami Seaquarium nearby.

SPLENDID CHINA

Splendid China seemed to have everything going for it. It had the seemingly limitless backing of the Chinese government and a great location near Disney World. The Chinese government already had a similar attraction in Shenzhen that was a success, so it was thought a Florida version could not miss. A woman from Taiwan, Josephine Chen, visited the Chinese attraction and convinced Chinese officials to invest in Orlando. She planned a similar, elaborate park on seventy-five acres with more than sixty replicas made to one-tenth scale. There were also nearly sixty performers

Splendid China seemed to have everything going for it, including rich backers and a great location. But then reality set in, and the park closed.

who came from China. Construction began in 1989, and the park opened four years later. The displays included a replica of the Great Wall, which stretched half a mile.

The model of the Leshan Buddha was four stories tall. As the park opened, the Chinese government wanted complete control. Problems began almost immediately. Some of the performers began defecting, and the Chinese government was reluctant to allow more people to leave the country. Then, the protests began. In 1995, school groups began boycotting the park, and there were demonstrations inside the park. There were frequent changes in management and even talk of changing the name to Chinatown. By 1999, the park was losing $9 million a year, and a year later, it closed amid accusations of financial mismanagement. Without security, vandals set upon the park, and there was widespread damage. In 2009, the park was put up for sale. In 2013, the new owners tore down what remained of the attraction. It became the site for Jimmy Buffett's Margaritaville Resort.

MIRACLE STRIP AMUSEMENT PARK

James Lark opened the Miracle Strip Amusement Park in 1963 in Panama City Beach. It featured a wooden roller coaster named the Starliner—the first roller coaster built in Florida—and each year, rides were added, including the Sea Dragon swinging boat and a haunted castle. Lark opened the Shipwreck Island Waterpark across the street. For nearly four decades, it remained a popular attraction and led to the creation of other tourist stops

The Miracle Strip Amusement Park was a huge draw in Panama City Beach for four decades, but the land became more valuable for development than as an attraction.

nearby. It played a pivotal role in increasing family tourism in Panama City. The park was well maintained, and improvements were made throughout the 1990s. After 9/11, attendance dropped dramatically. It was increasing by 2004, but the sprawling land Lark owned had become more valuable than the park. As the season ended on Labor Day 2004, the park closed for the last time. It had seen twenty million visitors over forty-one years.

GHOST TOWN

J.E. Churchwell was responsible for bringing the tourists to Bay County as the founder of Long Beach Resort. He was born in Bay County in 1896 and was frugal and saved his money while working as a bank clerk. In 1929, the Hathaway Bridge was built, opening Panama City Beach to tourists.

In 1933, development along the beach began. In 1935, Churchwell used the few hundred dollars he had saved to buy 160 acres of beachfront property.

Ghost Town was built by J.E. Churchwell, the founder of Long Beach Resort. It lasted into the 1980s then became an RV park and a Walmart.

The price was low, because it was the middle of the Great Depression, and the land was considered worthless. He called his land Long Beach Resort, although there was little to the resort and the tourists were sparse. After World War II, Churchwell met with Walt Disney and was inspired to begin adding attractions. He opened a roller rink and dance floor, which drew young people. Other attractions were opening nearby, and Churchwell responded to the competition by opening Petticoat Junction Amusement Park and Ghost Town. In 1975, Hurricane Eloise leveled the early developments, although the amusement park held on for another decade. Ghost Town was a row of Old West buildings featuring shootouts on the main street. He began adding to the Wild West theme with a roller coaster and other rides to form Petticoat Junction. Although the attraction had no connection to the television show of the same name, it did feature an old-fashioned railroad.

The development was haphazard, and many thought it was tacky. Journalist Tom Fiedler wrote, "The Panama City Beach strip could serve as a model of how not to develop a natural resource....[T]he gorgeous beach has been mugged and gagged."

The park closed in 1984, and the train station became part of an RV park while much of the rest became a Walmart.

JUNGLE LAND

Florida has had many attractions with "Jungle" in the name. This one opened in 1966 in Panama City Beach, featuring alligators and an artificial volcano belching smoke. There was a Journey to the Center of the Earth attraction, which featured skeletons and lava pits. In the late 1970s, the attraction closed, and the land was purchased by Alvin's Island Tropical Department Store. The new owners kept the volcano and the smoke.

OCEAN WORLD

When it opened in 1965 in Fort Lauderdale, this attraction featured "The Flying Dolphin Show," along with alligators, tropical birds and other creatures. In the 1980s, the park became a target for animal rights activists, which led to an investigation by the U.S. Department of Agriculture and a

$20,000 fine. The bigger problems included declining visitors, lack of room to expand, mounting financial losses and ever-increasing real estate values. The two hundred animals were relocated to other attractions.

OSTRICH FARM

Beginning in the late 1890s, ostrich farms became popular attractions. In 1885, Edwin Cawston chartered a ship to bring fifty ostriches from Africa to Texas, then to California. The eighteen that survived the journey soon began multiplying, and Cawston decided to open a second farm in Jacksonville. It opened in 1898 and quickly became a major attraction. An

The St. Augustine Alligator Farm was one of the first Florida attractions and one of the rare attractions to survive all of the competition.

ostrich can run up to forty-five miles an hour, and soon there were ostrich races. Riders could use a small carriage hooked to the ostrich or put a saddle on the ostrich. By 1912, the farm had outgrown its park and moved to larger quarters. When Dixieland Amusement Park opened in 1907, the two parks began competing for visitors. At first, Dixieland seemed to be the one to prevail, but by 1916, Dixieland was fading, and in the 1920s, the Ostrich Farm took over its site. By the 1930s, the park's popularity had faded, and it closed. The animals were purchased by the St. Augustine Alligator Farm in 1937.

SPANISH VILLAGE

In 1559, Tristán de Luna's expedition established Pensacola, the first European settlement in what is now the United States. In 1959, city officials

To celebrate its 400th anniversary, Pensacola built a model Spanish village, with artisans displaying work from the early Spanish rule.

celebrated the 400th anniversary by building a model Spanish village. It was based on a woodcut showing the Spanish village on Santa Rose Island.

Spanish artisans were stationed throughout the village to display their work utilizing tools from four centuries ago. The interiors featured period furniture. By 1973, the structures had deteriorated to the point that they were unfit for tourists. The buildings were razed.

Sulphur Springs

In 1900, J.H. Mills purchased Sulphur Springs north of the Hillsborough River near Tampa. For decades, it had been visited by people seeking its "healing waters." Mills added a dance pavilion, Ferris wheel and swimming pool. Eventually, there was a toboggan slide, alligator farm and arcade. In 1926, the Sulphur Springs Hotel opened. A year later, the iconic Sulphur Springs Water Tower was built. The springs became known as Florida's Coney Island. Tampa annexed the springs in 1953, and the problems began, as the city drew excessive amounts of water from the springs and pollution increased. The hotel was torn down for a parking lot, and today the springs are considered too polluted for swimming.

The Garden of Eden

The community of Bristol is located near the Georgia-Florida line. Even though it is the county seat of Liberty County, it has a population of only one thousand. In the 1950s, a minister named Elvy Callaway decided that the area around Bristol matched the biblical description of the Garden of Eden.

According to Callaway, the Apalachicola-Chattahoochee River system has four heads, just like in the Bible. He claimed that the area was rich in gopher wood, which Noah used to build the ark. Bristol became a minor tourist attraction for about twenty years as people came to see what Callaway claimed was the home of Adam and Eve.

The Reverend Elvy Callaway was convinced that the Garden of Eden was in the Florida Panhandle. He drew tourists who came to see where Callaway said Adam and Eve lived.

MUSEUM OF THE SEA AND INDIAN

The museum near Destin contained a mix of Indian artifacts and hundreds of shells. Outside, there were totem poles with holes for people to put their faces in for photos. The building was not air-conditioned and by the 1990s was clearly in decline. The museum was destroyed by Hurricane Opal in 1995.

TIKI GARDENS

Like scores of attractions, Frank and Jo Byars's started with a gift shop in Indian Shores and expanded it into Tiki Gardens. Frank owned four acres with palm trees, grass huts and painted stucco tiki statues. By 1969, the couple had expanded to a dozen acres with monkeys, birds and a restaurant. In 1986, they sold the attraction to foreign investors, who planned to build a hotel. Those plans fell through, and in 1990, the county purchased the land for $3 million. The county razed the buildings and sold the huge tiki sign to build a parking lot to give access to Tiki Gardens Beach.

U.S.A. OF YESTERDAY

The location seemed ideal: along the popular US 27 between Cypress Gardens and Walt Disney World. U.S.A. of Yesterday opened as Disney World was opening, and like dozens of other attraction owners, Earl Smith hoped there would be enough overflow to fill his museum. His collection included a 1931 Packard Roadster along with other early American mechanical inventions. The museum failed to attract tourists, and the property was sold for redevelopment.

CASPER'S OSTRICH AND ALLIGATOR FARM

In 1934, James Casper started a commercial gator farm, and in 1946, he started admitting tourists on US 1 about three miles from downtown St. Augustine. He had thousands of alligators and tropical birds, and he featured ostrich racing. Unfortunately, he was competing with another gator farm nearby. It closed in 1982, with the sixteen-foot concrete alligator going to Jacksonville's Metropolitan Park.

HOUSE OF MYSTERY

The House of Mystery was three miles north of Haines City, located on US 17/92, known as the Orange Blossom Trail. Other attractions, including Cypress Gardens, were nearby. It was popular in the 1950s, until Interstate 4 and Florida's Turnpike opened, causing traffic on 17/92 to dwindle to a trickle. All that was left was a road sign: Mystery House Road.

WET 'N WILD

In a business where having one success is unusual, George Millay had two. He started out in the restaurant business, and after selling out his interest in more than one hundred restaurants, he had the idea to open an underwater zoo. He and his partners came up with SeaWorld. The first opened in 1964 in San Diego. In 1973, SeaWorld Orlando opened, and four years later, Millay came up with the idea for Wet 'n Wild. The first year was difficult, and the investors lost $600,000. After that, every year was profitable and led to other Wet 'n Wild parks opening across the country. It was the most successful water park in the country until Walt Disney opened Typhoon Lagoon and Blizzard Beach. Universal Studios Florida purchased Wet 'n Wild in 2013, although it was primarily interested in the fifty acres it controlled. Universal opened its own water park, Volcano Bay, and closed Wet 'n Wild in 2016 to make room for a four-thousand-room hotel.

KLASSIX AUTO MUSEUM

When it opened in 1994, Klassix Auto Museum seemed to have everything going for it. It was near the Daytona International Speedway, which seemed to guarantee that it would be a draw for the hundreds of thousands of

Above: James Casper started his gator farm in 1934 and eventually had thousands of alligators. But he could not overcome a nearby competitor and closed the park in 1982.

Right: The House of Mystery was on a popular tourist route before the interstate highway and Florida's Turnpike came in and attendance declined.

With the ambulance from *Ghostbusters* and a Corvette from every model year, Klassix Auto Museum seemed certain of success. But after a decade, the attraction closed.

racing fans who attend events each year. It certainly had the cars, including a Corvette from every model year, stock cars and motorcycles. Two years after opening, driver Mark Martin came on board, and the museum was renamed Mark Martin's Klassix Auto Museum. But it didn't help, and the museum closed in 2003. Many of the vehicles were auctioned off, including one of the five classic Batmobiles, which sold for $172,500; the ambulance from *Ghostbusters* ($55,000); and Jed Clampett's truck from the film *The Beverly Hillbillies* ($31,000).

FAIRYLAND

In the 1930s, a zoo opened in Tampa with a collection of readily available animals, including alligators, raccoons and exotic birds. Gradually, more animals were added until it was a real zoo. Admission was free, and Sheena the elephant performed twice a day and gave rides to children. In 1957, the city announced plans to build a children's park similar to one in New Orleans.

Fairyland was built for children and featured storybook characters. To enter, visitors slid into the park on Rainbow Bridge. There was a railroad and a zoo next door. When more land was needed for the zoo, Fairyland closed.

Tampa called its park Fairyland, and it was loaded with familiar characters, including Little Red Riding Hood, Humpty Dumpty and Little Miss Muffet. City officials said entry to Fairyland would be across the Rainbow Bridge, which would have children slide into the land. Concrete replicas of the figures were built, along with a barn for the Little Red Horn, a giant shoe for the Old Lady and a castle with a moat.

Fairyland was designed for Tampa children, but it became an attraction drawing visitors from throughout the country. Some rides were added, including the Fairyland Railroad. Combined with the zoo next door, it could be a day's worth of entertainment for a modest price.

In the late 1990s, the city needed more space for the zoo, and the concrete figures were showing their age. The Rainbow Bridge was deemed unsafe and torn down. The figures were sent to a city warehouse, and the rides were auctioned off in 1997.

After twenty years of neglect, efforts began to rehabilitate the figures and put them around town.

Miami Aquarium

James Allison was a partner with Carl Fisher in the Prest-O-Lite company, inventors of the automobile headlight. Together they became rich and used their money to build the Indianapolis Motor Speedway.

When they sold their company to Union Carbide, they became multimillionaires. The two moved to Florida and began developing Miami Beach. In 1919, Allison turned his attention to building an aquarium to serve as a research facility and a tourist attraction. It opened on New Year's Day 1921 featuring only fish caught within fifty miles of Miami.

The aquarium was a good draw but lost more money than Allison could afford. There were attempts to get the city to take over the attraction, but no help came. After three years, the aquarium was closed and the fish sent to the Detroit Aquarium or released into the Caribbean. The building was torn down, and a high-end hotel was erected.

Six Gun Territory

In the late 1950s and early 1960s, Western-themed television shows ruled the airwaves. In 1959, there were thirty Western television programs in prime time.

Florida attractions wanted to cash in. There was Pioneer City in South Florida, Tombstone Territory in the Panhandle and Fort Dodge in Brooksville.

Six Gun Territory was the biggest, built on 250 acres and opened in 1963. Unlike many parks, which featured only the façades of building, Sun Gun Territory could have been a real Western town. There were shootouts and bank robberies, can-can dancers at the Palace Saloon and a real, old-fashioned train. The park was an immediate success, as tourists could visit Silver Springs and nearby Six Gun Territory in one trip.

But the Western television shows were canceled; Disney World, EPCOT and SeaWorld opened; and Six Gun Territory attendance declined. It closed in 1984. The land became a shopping center named Six Gun Plaza.

The Aquarium, Miami, Fla.

James Allison is largely forgotten today, but along with Carl Fisher he invented the automobile headlight then helped develop Miami Beach. In 1919, he built an aquarium with fish caught within fifty miles of Miami. It lost more money than he could afford and closed after three years.

Six Gun Territory joined the list of Western-themed attractions opening in Florida in the mid-1950s. Six Gun Territory was the best, with real buildings and a large cast. But it could not compete with Disney and closed in 1984.

THE GREAT MASTERPIECE

No Florida attraction has had a more dramatic history than The Great Masterpiece. In 1929, the August Wagner Company in Berlin made a three-hundred-thousand-piece mosaic of da Vinci's *Last Supper*. As the Nazis came to power in Germany, high-ranking government officials began looting the art of Europe.

The owners of the mosaic worried that their work would be stolen, and they hid the work. As the war went on, they thought it might fall victim to bombing or capture by the advancing Russian army.

The Great Masterpiece had a dramatic history, hidden from the Nazis and smuggled out of Germany. The mosaic was a good draw until traffic on US 27 dwindled.

At the end of the war, the work, weighing five thousand pounds, was brought to the United States and found a home in Lake Wales, where it was assembled over a two-year period.

The Great Masterpiece, Cypress Gardens and the Bok Tower were known as the big three of Florida tourism.

In the 1950s, it was a great draw, but by the 1960s, attendance slumped and the park added a train ride, sky ride and animal shows, including alligators. It helped a bit, but in the 1970s, there were more additions, including Monkey Island, deer feeding and a name change to Masterpiece Gardens.

In 1981, the rides were auctioned, and a religious organization acquired the land and gave the mosaic to a private college.

KEY DATES IN FLORIDA TOURISM

1878   Hullam Jones puts a pane of glass in the bottom of a boat to help him spot underwater logs in Silver Springs and invents the classic glass-bottom boat.

1893   The St. Augustine Alligator Farm is opened.

1897   A.J. Richardson moves to Miami and starts what becomes the Musa Isle Fruit Farm.

1910   "Alligator Joe" Frazee opens an alligator farm in Miami.

1911   Henry Coppinger starts Coppinger's Tropical Gardens in Miami.

1914   Tony Janus starts the world's first airline, flying passengers from St. Petersburg to Tampa. Three airlines, National, Eastern and Pan American, all start in Florida.

1916   Construction on the magnificent mansion Viscaya is completed in Miami.

1924   Carl Ray and W.M. Davidson purchase the land for Silver Springs Park.

1925   Construction on the Tamiami Trail begins, connecting Tampa with Miami. The 273-mile road is completed in 1928.

1925   George T. Christie purchases Wakulla Springs and begins development and glass-bottom boat tours.

1927   Maud and Charlie Black turn their gas station and home in South Miami into a popular tourist stop. The couple makes coconut candy the main attraction and draws a steady stream of customers until 1939. Their home featured a large sausage tree, and they called their stop Charlie Black's Sausage Tree.

1929   Bok Tower Gardens in Lake Wales is dedicated by President Calvin Coolidge.

1930   Davis Aloe Vera Tropical Gardens opens in Homestead. It featured tropical plants and sold "Medicine Aloe." It closed in 1937.

1934   Key West Aquarium is built. George Christie sells Wakulla Spring to Edward Ball. Bull Frog Farm opens in Dania. Throughout the 1930s, scores of frog farms opened in the United States. The idea was that people could make money raising and selling frogs. During the Great Depression, it attracted hundreds, perhaps thousands, of eager investors. In Dania, visitors could see frogs for ten cents and sample frog legs. It turned out that there was a frog bubble, which collapsed, and Bull Frog Farm closed after three years. Daytona Beach Alligator Farm closed after moving from Jacksonville. When it closed in 1942, the alligator collection was acquired by the St. Augustine Alligator Farm.

1935   Sunken Gardens opens in St. Petersburg, and Monkey Jungle opens in Miami.

1936   Everglades Wonder Gardens opens in Bonita Springs, Cypress Gardens opens in Winter Haven and Parrot Jungle opens in Miami.

1937   Rattlesnake Headquarters opens in Tampa after moving from
        Arcadia.

1937   Oriental Gardens opens in Jacksonville. In 1925, George Clark
        began planting beautiful flowers and shrubs and after a decade
        opened it to the public. There were hourly concerts and one
        hundred varieties of tropical and subtropical plants. In 1954,
        the site was purchased by developers, who carved it into thirty-
        three homesites.

1937   Billy's Seminole Indian Village opens in Hobe Sound near
        Stuart.

1938   Winter Park Scenic Boat Tour begins tours. Brook's Tropical
        Wyldewood Nursery opens in Dania. It became Wyldewood
        Bird Farm and lasted until 1959.

1939   Clyde Beatty's Jungle Zoo opens in Fort Lauderdale. Marine
        Zoo opens in St. Petersburg and closes three years later. Tarzan
        Park in Vero Beach opens. It was a fraud based on a fact. In
        1913, vertebrate fossils were uncovered near the Indian River.
        Two years later, twenty-six fossilized human bones were found.
        A debate arose over their age and significance. In 1939, Tarzan
        Park opened, and for twenty-five cents visitors could see "Vero
        Man" and other human and animal remains. While the earlier
        finds were genuine, the ones in Tarzan Park were a hoax. The
        park closed in 1942.

1940   Sarasota Jungle Gardens opens and Dupree Gardens opens in
        Land O' Lakes. Earl Gresh opens his Wood Parade Museum
        in St. Petersburg. Sarasota Jungle Gardens opens. The City of
        St. Petersburg acquires Weeki Wachee Springs as a potential
        future water source for the city. Guinea Pig Colony opens in St.
        Petersburg. It claimed to have the world's largest collection of
        guinea pigs, which proved to be an underwhelming draw and
        closed after two years.

1941   Japanese attack on Pearl Harbor. Initially, tourism takes a
        serious hit, but the tourists are soon replaced by soldiers as the

state becomes a major training site for hundreds of thousands of soldiers.

1944   George End, the founder of Rattlesnake Headquarters, dies from a rattlesnake bite, and his attraction is closed.

1945   Clyde Beatty's Jungle Zoo closes.

1946   Theater of the Sea opens in Islamorada and becomes one of Florida's longest-surviving family-owned attractions. Riviera Tropical Gardens opens in South Miami. It began as a nursery business but began charging admission to see its plants and trees. It closed in 1951. Snake-A-Torium opens in Panama City Beach. Jack Tillman operated the attraction for eight years then sold it to Dennie Sebolt, who milked rattlesnakes and added alligators, tropical birds and bears. He sold the property in 1991, and it became Zoo World. It has expanded and added hundreds of animals.

1947   Thomas Edison's Fort Myers estate opens to the public. It was donated by his widow. Weeeki Wachee Spring opens its live underwater mermaid show. President Harry Truman dedicates Everglades National Park. Alma Cagle opens Alma and Her Snakes in Marathon. Her snakes and the gift shop were a popular attraction and lasted until 1959. Caswell's Orchid Garden opens in a home near downtown St. Petersburg. With little overhead, it lasted until 1965.

1948   The Lightner Museum opens in St. Augustine. The House of Mystery opens in Dunedin. It moved to St. Augustine a few years later and closed in 1956.

1949   Snake Village and Alligator Farm open near Kissimmee. They later become Gatorland.

1950   Ripley's Museum opens in St. Augustine.

1951   Africa U.S.A. opens in Boca Raton.

1952   The Great Masterpiece (Masterpiece Gardens) opens in Lake Wales.

1953   Ancient America opens in Boca Raton. Cars of Yesterday opens in Sarasota.

1955   Gulfarium opens in Fort Walton Beach. Miami Seaquarium opens in Miami. Storyland opens in Pompano Beach.

1956   Circus Hall of Fame opens in Sarasota. Aquafair opens in Miami.

1957   Gatorama opens in Palmdale, and Florida Citrus Tower opens in Clermont.

1959   Sunshine Springs and Gardens in Sarasota closes. Miami Wax Museum opens in Miami. Busch Gardens opens at the site of a Budweiser plant in Tampa.

Sunshine Springs and Gardens featured a swan boat ride through tropical gardens in Sarasota. It lasted from 1955 to 1959.

1960   Clyde Beatty buys Aquafair and turns it into Jungleland, but it lasts just one year. Bazaar International and Trylon Tower open in Riviera Beach.

1961   Africa U.S.A. closes.

1963   Six Gun Territory opens in Ocala. Tussaud's London Wax Museum opens in St. Petersburg. Crisswell's Money Museum opens in St. Petersburg Beach.

1964   Storyland closes. Aquatarium opens in St. Petersburg Beach. Cape Coral Gardens opens. Floridaland opens in Osprey.

1965   International Swimming Hall of Fame opens in Fort Lauderdale. *The Cross and Sword* premieres in St. Augustine. Texas Jim's Sarasota Reptile Farm and Zoo closes.

1966   Pioneer City opens in Fort Lauderdale.

1967   Pirates World opens in Dania, and Lion Country Safari opens in West Palm Beach.

1970   McLarty Treasure Museum opens in Sebastian Inlet.

1971   Walt Disney's Magic Kingdom opens in Orlando.

1973   SST Aviation Exhibit opens near Orlando. Marco Polo Park opens in Bunnell.

1974   Six Flags Stars Hall of Fame opens in Orlando.

1976   Reptile World Serpentarium opens to the public in St. Cloud. Mystery Fun House opens in Orlando.

1978   The Ocean Opry opens in Panama City Beach. Marco Polo Park is sold at auction. Wild Waters opens at Silver Springs.

1979   Fun 'n Wheels opens in Orlando.

Jim Mitchell operated his alligator farm from 1935 to 1965 in Sarasota.

1981   Masterpiece Gardens (The Great Masterpiece) closes. SST Museum closes. The planes and vehicles at the defunct Wings and Wheels Museum in Orland are sold at auction.

1982   EPCOT opens in Orlando. Buccaneer Bay opens in Weeki Wachee. The Salvador Dalí Museum opens in St. Petersburg.

1983   Medieval Times/ Dinner Tournament opens outside Orlando.

1984   Miami Wax Museum closes, as do Miami Serpentarium, Six Gun Territory and Petticoat Junction.

1985   Pirate Island in Fort Walton Beach closes.

1987   Circus World becomes Boardwalk and Baseball. Fort Liberty opens in Kissimmee.

1988   Flying Tigers Warbird Restoration Museum opens in Kissimmee. Arabian Nights opens in Orlando.

1989   Disney/MGM Studios in Orlando opens. Tussaud's London Wax Museum closes.

1990   Boardwalk and Baseball closes. Astronaut Hall of Fame opens in Titusville. Universal Studios opens in Orlando. The Florida Sports Hall of Fame opens in Lake City. It began in Cypress Gardens in 1977, then moved to Lake City in 1990.

1992   Ripley's Believe It or Not! opens in Orlando.

1993   The World of Orchids opens in Kissimmee. Splendid China opens near Kissimmee.

1994   Klassix Auto Museum opens in Daytona Beach. Ocean World in Fort Lauderdale closes.

1995   The Top O' the Strip Observation Tower in Panama City is demolished.

1996   *The Cross and Sword* closes. Daytona USA opens at Daytona International Speedway. The International Museum of Cartoon Art opens in Boca Raton.

1997   Skull Kingdom opens in Orlando.

1998   The Black Hills Passion Play closes. Wonderworks opens in Orlando. The Tragedy in US History Museum closes. Animal Kingdom opens in Orlando.

1999   Titanic: The Exhibition opens in Orlando. Universal Studios Islands of Adventure opens in Orlando. Sunken Gardens in St. Petersburg closes and becomes a city park.

2000   Cypress Knee Museum closes.

2001   Mystery Fun House closes. The Holy Land Experience opens in Orlando.

2002   Guinness World Records Experience closes, as does the International Museum of Cartoon Art.

2003   Cypress Gardens closes, as does Florida Splendid China.

2004   The Miracle Strip Amusement Park closes, as does the Hard Rock Vault.

2005   The Ocean Opry closes, as does Water Mania. Xanadu: Home of the Future is demolished.

2006   The Ted Williams Museum and Hitters Hall of Fame closes in Hernando and moves to Tropicana Field in St. Petersburg. Skull Kingdom closes.

2009   SeaWorld's Aquatica water park opens in Orlando.

2010   The Wizarding World of Harry Potter opens at Universal Studios.

2011   Wannado City closes in Sunrise.

2012   "The Senator," a giant cypress tree thought to be 3,500 years old, burns down in Longwood, the result of arson.

2014   Arabian Nights Dinner Attraction closes.

2016   Wet 'n Wild closes.

LOST ATTRACTIONS BY DATE

Attraction	City	Dates
Cypress Gardens	Winter Haven	1936–2009
Bird Island Sanctuary	Orange Lake	1936–74
Wonder House	Bartow	1936–63
Oriental Gardens	Jacksonville	1937–39
Rainbow Springs	Dunnellon	1937–74
Dupree Gardens	Tampa	1940–54
Casper's Ostrich & Alligator Farm	St. Augustine	1946–82
Snake-A-Torium	Panama City	1946–96
Suwannee River Jungle Drive	Old Town	1946–72
Riviera Tropical Gardens	South Miami	1946–49
Chimp Farm	Dania	1946–56
Sarasota Reptile Farm & Zoo	Sarasota	1947–68
Midget City	Sanford	1947–56
Idlywyld Gardens	Winter Haven	1947–52
Anirama	Miami	1947–50
Miami Serpentarium	Miami	1948–84
Florida Wild Animal Farm	Callahan	1948–60
Paradise Park	Silver Springs	1949–56

The Suwannee River Jungle Drive took visitors along the Suwannee River in an old-fashioned horse-drawn carriage.

Attraction	City	Dates
Bongoland	South Daytona	1949–52
Florida Reptile Gardens	Flagler Beach	1950–56
Florida Reptile Land	Lawtey	1950–75
Eastern Garden Aquarium	Kendall	1950–57
Great Masterpiece	Lake Wales	1951–78
Cypress Knee Museum	Palmdale	1951–93
Sea Zoo	South Daytona	1951–70
Africa U.S.A.	Boca Raton	1953–61
Autorama	Hypoluxo	1953–61
Ancient America	Boca Raton	1953–58
Carriage Cavalcade	Silver Springs	1953–77
John's Pass Aquarium	Madeira Beach	1953–65
Fort Greggs Animal Compound	St. Augustine	1954–66
Sea-Orama	Clearwater Beach	1954–68
Moonshine Still	St. Augustine	1954–60
Everglades Tropical Gardens	Clewiston	1954–75

Attraction	City	Dates
Tommy Bartlett's Deer Ranch	Silver Springs	1954–76
Museum of Speed	South Daytona	1954–77
Atomic Tunnel	Port Orange	1954–60
Sunshine Springs and Gardens	Sarasota	1955–59
Turner's River Jungle Cruise	Ochopee	1956–63
Parrot Village	Ormond Beach	1956–71
Storyland	Pompano Beach	1956–62
Seminole Reptile Gardens	Stuart	1956–61
Tropical Panorama	North Miami	1956–60
Circus Hall of Fame	Sarasota	1956–60
Everglades Wildlife Park	Punta Gorda	1956–77
Aquaglades Park	Fort Lauderdale	1958–71

The Carriage Cavalcade was one of the attractions at Silver Springs. It featured vehicles ranging from horse-drawn carriages to early automobiles. It opened in 1953 and closed in 1977.

People think of Florida as sun and fun, but few realize that it is known for its phosphate mines. Phosphate is used to make fertilizer, and Florida is a major producer. The industry decided to open an attraction, but few tourists came, and it closed after a dozen years.

Attraction	City	Dates
Animal Land	St. Augustine	1958–67
Neptune's Garden	Marathon	1959–63
Museum of the Sea and Indian	Destin	1959–94
Birds of Prey	Lake Wales	1959–71
Frog City	Tamiami Trail	1960–92
Dog Land	Chiefland	1960–74
Tarpon Zoo & Animal Compound	Tarpon Springs	1961–75
Rainforest	Sumterville	1961–67
Phosphate Valley Exposition	Bartow	1961–73
Foxbower Wildlife Museum	Brooksville	1961–80
Okalee Indian Village	Dania	1962–78
Fort Dodge	Brooksville	1962–66
Cape Coral Gardens	Cape Coral	1968–77

BIBLIOGRAPHY

Adams, John R. *Harriet Beecher Stowe*. Boston: Twayne Publishers, 1989.

Akin, Edward N. *Flagler: Rockefeller Partner and Florida Baron*. Gainesville: University Press of Florida, 1992.

Aron, Cindy Sondik. *Working at Play: A History of Vacations in the United States*. New York: Oxford University Press, 2001.

Arsenault, Raymond. "The End of the Long Hot Summer: The Air Conditioner and Southern Culture." *Journal of Southern History* 50, no. 4 (1984): 597.

Barnes, Jay. *Florida's Hurricane History*. Chapel Hill: University of North Carolina Press, 2007.

Bass, Bob. *When Steamboats Reigned in Florida*. Gainesville: University Press of Florida, 2008.

Belasco, Warren James. *Americans on the Road: From Autocamp to Motel, 1910–1945*. Baltimore, MD: Johns Hopkins University Press, 1997.

Belleville, Bill. *River of Lakes: A Journey on Florida's St. Johns River*. Athens: University of Georgia Press, 2018.

Bolton, Herbert Eugene. *The Spanish Borderlands*. Norman: University of Oklahoma Press, 1974.

Braden, Susan R. *Architecture of Leisure: The Florida Resort Hotels of Henry Flagler and Henry Plant*. Gainesville: University Press of Florida, 2018.

Branch, Stephen E. "The Salesman and His Swamp: Dick Pope's Cypress Gardens." *Florida Historical Quarterly* 80 (Spring 2002): 483–503.

Breslauer, Ken. *Roadside Paradise: The Golden Age of Florida's Tourist Attractions: 1929–1971*. St. Petersburg: RetroFlorida, 2000.

Clark, James C. *Concise History of Florida*. Charleston, SC: The History Press, 2014.

Covington, James W. *The Seminoles of Florida*. Gainesville: University Press of Florida, 2017.

Covington, James W., and Tommy L. Thompson. *Plant's Palace: Henry B. Plant and the Tampa Bay Hotel*. Louisville, KY: Harmony House Publishers, 1991.

Derr, Mark. *Some Kind of Paradise: A Chronicle of Man and the Land in Florida*. Gainesville: University Press of Florida, 1998.

"Florida's Lost Tourist Attractions." Florida's Lost Tourist Attractions. http://lostparks.com.

Foglesong, Richard E. *Married to the Mouse: Walt Disney World and Orlando*. New Haven, CT: Yale University Press, 2003.

Foster, John T., and Sarah Whitmer Foster. *Beechers, Stowes, and Yankee Strangers: The Transformation of Florida*. Gainesville: University Press of Florida, 1999.

Gabler, Neal. *Walt Disney: The Triumph of the American Imagination*. New York: Knopf, 2008.

Hollis, Tim. *Dixie before Disney: 100 Years of Roadside Fun*. Oxford: University Press of Mississippi, 1999.

———. *Florida's Miracle Strip: From Redneck Riviera to Emerald Coast*. Oxford: University Press of Mississippi, 2004.

———. *Glass Bottom Boats & Mermaid Tails: Florida's Tourist Springs*. Mechanicsburg, PA: Stackpole Books, 2006.

Johns, John E. *Florida during the Civil War*. Gainesville: University Press of Florida, 1989.

Kilby, Rick. *Florida's Healing Waters: Gilded Age Mineral Springs, Seaside Resorts, and Health Spas*. Gainesville: University Press of Florida, 2020.

Lanier, Sidney, and Jerrell H. Shofner. *Florida: Its Scenery, Climate, and History*. Gainesville: University Press of Florida, 1976.

Ledyard, Bill. *Winter in Florida*. New York: Wood & Holbrook, 1870.

Lee, Henry. *The Tourist's Guide of Florida*. New York: Leve & Alden Print Company, 1885.

Mormino, Gary. "Roadsides and Broadsides: A History of Florida Tourism." *Forum* 10, Fall 1987.

Mormino, Gary Ross. *Land of Sunshine, State of Dreams: A Social History of Modern Florida*. Gainesville: University Press of Florida, 2008.

Ogle, Maureen. *Key West: History of an Island of Dreams*. Gainesville: University Press of Florida, 2018.

"185 Lost Florida Tourist Attractions: Fun While They Lasted." Gainesville: Florida Back Roads Travel. https://www.florida-backroads-travel.com/lost-attractions.html.

Patrick, Rembert Wallace. *Florida under Five Flags*. Gainesville: University Press of Florida, 1965.

Preston, Howard L. *Dirt Roads to Dixie: Accessibility and Modernization in the South, 1885–1935*. Knoxville: University of Tennessee Press, 1991.

"Rambler." Pseud. *Guide to Florida*. New York: American News Company, 1875.

Revels, Tracy J. *Sunshine Paradise: A History of Florida Tourism*. Gainesville: University Press of Florida, 2020.

INDEX

G

H

I

M

N

ABOUT THE AUTHOR

James C. Clark is a senior lecturer at the University of Central Florida, where he directs the Florida Studies Program. He is the author of twelve books on Florida history, including *Florida: A Concise History*, and the editor of a three-volume anthology of Florida literature. He earned his doctorate in Florida history at the University of Florida. His work has been honored by the Florida Historical Society, the Florida Magazine Association and the Florida Society of Newspaper Editors. He lives in Orlando.